NINE SHORT PLAYS

BY CAROLYN GAGE

Outskirts Press, Inc.
Denver, Colorado

Nine Short Plays
All Rights Reserved.
Copyright © 2008 Carolyn Gage
V2.0

Front and back cover paintings by Sudie Rakusin 2007 www.sudierakusin.com

Outskirts Press, Inc.
http://www.outskirtspress.com

ISBN: 978-1-4327-2025-4

Outskirts Press and the "OP" logo are trademarks belonging to Outskirts Press, Inc.

PRINTED IN THE UNITED STATES OF AMERICA

Other Books by Carolyn Gage

The Second Coming of Joan of Arc and Other Plays
Take Stage! How to Direct and Produce a Lesbian Play
Monologues and Scenes for Lesbian Actors
*Like There's No Tomorrow: Meditations for Women
    Leaving Patriarchy*
Like a Lover: Daily Readings for a Women's Revolution

Praise for Carolyn Gage

"The culture of women we have never had is invented in Carolyn Gage's brilliant and beautiful plays."—**Andrea Dworkin, feminist philosopher activist, and author**

"The work of an experienced and esteemed playwright like Carolyn Gage is the air that modern theatre needs."—**Jewelle Gomez, author of *The Gilda Stories*, San Francisco Arts Commissioner**

"...the toughest, most lesbian/feminist-identified work for theatre I know . . . brilliant and daring scripts . . ." —**John Stoltenberg, former Executive Editor, *On the Issues*, and author of *Refusing to Become a Man***

"Carolyn Gage's writing, acting, and teaching are explosive. She rips away the cultural camouflage that permits us to accept, to be blind to, the brutal context in which women are still required to live their lives." —**Prof. George Wolf, Dept. of English, University of Nebraska, Lincoln**

"I know of no living playwright who is grappling with issues as controversial and as central to the survival of our people as Carolyn Gage. Possibly the most potentially transformative work of our time is the work on trauma conducted by psychologists and academics as well as within feminist and recovery movements. By joining her intellectual and political engagements with these movements to her considerable skills as a dramatist, Gage creates plays that bring the "magic" back to theatre."—**Dr. Patricia Cramer, Dept. of English, University of Connecticut, Stamford**

"Carolyn will bring…not only her incredibly prolific theatrical repertoire but also the richness of her intellect and astute political comprehension of women's lives and the necessity of our struggle—of all people's struggles—against the colonization of our minds and bodies. She has a great gift and the ability to synthesize the truths of women's lives and to tell them without shrinking from their pain and complexity."—**Julia Penelope, co-editor of** *The Original Coming Out Stories, For Lesbians Only*, **and** *Lesbian Culture: An Anthology*

"Carolyn Gage is a national lesbian treasure."
—**Rosemary Keefe Curb, editor of** *Amazon All Stars: 13 Lesbian Plays*

Nine Short Plays

by Carolyn Gage

Nine Short Plays

Gage Press

Contents

Introduction

This is a collection of nine very different plays that, among other things, explores the impact of the dominant culture on intimate relationships.

In *The Obligatory Scene,* a young lesbian couple finds that the very gender roles that brought them together have become the primary obstacle to their intimacy. *Bite My Thumb* takes a more swashbuckling approach to gender roles, focusing on who gets to play—or fight—and who is assigned the supporting roles.

In *Entr'acte,* a young Eva Le Gallienne struggles, in the aftermath of a backstage rape by an unnamed assailant, with her former partner—a woman who abandoned both Eva and her acting career for the security of a heterosexual marriage. *The Pele Chant* explores the spiritual colonization of Hawaii through the eyes of Queen Liliuokalani's adopted daughter—a woman who chose life partnership with a white woman over a traditional marriage.

Louisa May Incest asks, "What happens when a writer creates a character who is more evolved than her creator?" A similar confrontation occurs in *Jane Addams and the Devil Baby*, where the privileged and lesbian Addams struggles to understand the experience of a woman whose entire life experience has been shaped by the constrictions of compulsory heterosexuality. In *Patricide*, where the oppression is internalized, the dialogue has become a monologue.

Battered on Broadway and *The Rules of the Playground* are both satires about women's collusion with cultural and political institutions that marginalize our roles and silence our protest.

These nine plays reflect my fascination with the ways in which political paradigms are reflected in interpersonal dynamics, and especially how internalized oppression can mask itself as a strategy for liberation, when, it fact, it is a Trojan Horse for the forces that would destroy us.

My *modus operandi* is to tell a story wherein the character's irresistible impulse, usually toward some form of freedom, is checked by a seemingly immoveable force of society. If the characters have enough integrity and the situation enough authenticity, I find myself, at least for a while, wrestling with angels or demons. And then there is a break-through, a shift into another paradigm, where radical possibility abounds. This is why I write.

The Obligatory Scene

Martha Graham wrote in her autobiography *Blood Memory*, "In many ways, I showed onstage what most people came to the theatre to avoid."

In *The Obligatory Scene*, I wanted to address an aspect of lesbian intimacy that is frequently closeted; namely, the fact that, in many relationships, and especially those involving survivors of sexual abuse, one of the partners will become unwilling or unable to participate in sex.

Studies on lesbian sexuality have documented that the average lesbian relationship becomes asexual after about two years. This is an interesting statistic, because lesbian cultural representations would give the impression that lesbian couples are on permanent honeymoon in terms of our sexuality. Our community, especially since its contamination by a male-dominated, queer culture, has become aggressively identified with sexual practices, sexual paraphernalia, sexual role-playing, and so on. Who are these couples with no sex life, and how are they coping with the onslaught of sexual propaganda that characterizes our films, our novels, our poetry, our theatre, our magazines, and our festivals?

The traditional scenario requires that the partner who has developed an aversion to sex be identified as "in need of healing." The other partner then "support-ively" waits an appropriate amount of time for her partner to seek therapy and "heal her sexuality." If this so-called healing is not forthcoming, the partner, having "tried to hang in there," will eventually leave the relationship for greener pastures. Greener, at least, for about two years, at which time her new partner—or perhaps herself—may lose interest, and the cycle begins again.

This story is so painful and so commonplace, lesbians tend not to talk about it. "The problem" appears to have no solution.

The Obligatory Scene is my attempt to confront this dynamic in a dramatic format, and to explore the possibility of an alternative, and radical, ending for the story. In this play, I want to suggest that the survivor in late-stage recovery who has become uncomfortable with sex may actually be onto something about intimacy that goes beyond sex-as-our-culture-defines-it. Turning the tables, my play suggests that it may be the "normal" partner who is in need of healing.

This play is not an argument against sexual intimacy. It is a plea for a deconstruction of what that currently means, and a reconstruction of it in terms of personally customized metaphors. Drawing from the recent work of therapists who work with survivors of sexual trauma, I wanted to end the play on a note of promise: There can be sexual healing, but the price of that healing is that both partners, not just the survivor, must be willing to start from scratch. The sexually active partner must be willing to interrogate her assumptions about what constitutes normal sexual practices, and the stigmatized partner must be willing to loosen some of her armor and begin to accept the possibility of an ally in what has been a private and protected, albeit trauma-bedeviled and stigmatized, space.

I open the play with a discussion of *Taming of the Shrew*, because it depicts a couple struggling to subvert a context of sexual subordination, even as they are compelled to enact roles dictated by that context. The playwright's attempt is, in fact, so subversive, he has had to encode the "obligatory scene" so that only the initiated could decipher the hidden meaning of the play.

Dru and Vivey, although lesbians, are still struggling with a legacy of toxic gender roles. No longer shackled by a social code as rigid as that imposed on Katharine and Petruchio, they yet find themselves hampered by lack of precedents. Vivey performs a fem sexuality in a political vacuum, while Dru is a prisoner of her post-traumatic associations. The "obligatory scene" for a couple in their situation is one they refuse to play: the inevitable break-up. Instead, they make a tentative commitment to abandon the roles that have comprised their survival strategies, opening up a space for new identities, new scripts, new languages of intimacy, and new and—one hopes—happier endings.

Bite My Thumb

This play was originally written in response to a call for plays by an all-women theatre company specializing in sword-fighting. Very quickly, the play evolved into a critique of companies like theirs that exploited the trendiness of "cute-girls-in-tights," cross-dressing roles from the classical repertory.

Much of my work explores the heavily censored role of the lesbian butch, and two decades of attempting to market, produce, and tour with these works has confirmed my suspicion that the reason for the resistance to this archetype lies in its indictment of traditional gender roles. The lesbian butch is living proof that qualities traditionally ascribed to "masculinity" are not innately linked to the Y chromosome. As an archetype, the lesbian butch demands a radical paradigm of gender, one that goes to the root of male dominance. The narrative that emerges from this archetype and paradigm is one of almost unimaginable liberation.

In *Bite My Thumb*, I began with the idea of two rival "gangs" of actors from competing productions of *Romeo and Juliet*, one of which was being done by an all-women company. This set-up provided the opportunity to explore all kinds of notions about gender and about fighting, against a backdrop of gender roles so familiar that "Romeo" and "Juliet" have come to represent the global epitome of a young, heterosexual, romantic couple.

In the play, the males challenge each other on notions of machismo, while the lesbian romantic couple has, unfortunately, replicated the traditional, casting-couch dynamic of mainstream, heterosexist theatre. Against these gendered roles, it is the female-to-male, transgendered actor and the lesbian butch who stand out as deviant.

Their marginal status is highlighted by their strategies for making a place for themselves in the heterosexist narrative: The transgendered male is passing in order to play Mercutio in the male-dominated company, while the lesbian butch in the all-women company has accepted the role of Juliet's nurse, a "character part" which mocks her non-traditional looks and desexualizes her.

In the course of all of the sword-fighting, it becomes apparent that it is "Mercutio" and the "Nurse" who are the real warriors—a status that will never be acknowledged in the world of mainstream drama. This exclusion becomes literal when they are each fired by their respective companies. Confronting this injustice, the two form a subversive bond that holds the promise of a new archetype in which the fierce warrior spirit is fused with the tender vulnerability of being woman-identified in a patriarchal rape culture.

Entr'acte,

or *The Night Eva Le Gallienne Was Raped*

I had been reading the biographies of Eva Le Gallienne, and the stories about her relationship with her father, suggestive of incest, caught my attention, as did the story of her rape during the run of *Liliom*. I had been using *Carousel*, the musical derived from *Liliom*, as an example of the misogyny of mainstream musicals for almost a decade at that point. I was also fascinated by Eva's lesbian relationship to former girlfriend Mimsey Benson. Mimsey was a decade older, had been understudying on Eva's tours, and broke up with Eva in order to marry a man. The rape occurred within a year of this abandonment.

I was intrigued with the intersection of all these vectors: the pro-rape themes of *Liliom*, the sexism that may have contributed to Mimsey's unusual choice, Eva's previous experience with her father, and, most of all, Eva's subsequent career as the founder and director of the Civic Repertory Theatre, a theatre with a mission so antithetical to that of the Broadway theatres.

The doll whose head was shattered and replaced, a gift from Eva's father, actually existed. There was a picture of it in one of the biographies. I could not have asked for a more perfect metaphor for dissociative identity disorders as a result of childhood trauma. In the play, I depict Eva "trying on different heads" as she switches rapidly from one manic state to another.

This play contains a map of recovery from trauma. There is the denial, the rage, the grief, the bargaining, and, finally, the acceptance. The rape has happened, and so has the abandonment by her lover. Mimsey is not coming back, and the show must go on. Furthermore, the rapes and abandonments will continue to happen on and off stage in the world of patriarchal theatre.

Eva comes to an understanding of the connection between her professional acting and her personal acting-out of misogynist scripts. After a long night of turmoil, as the light of a new day inexorably dawns, her denial finally dissipates. Like Shakespeare's Juliet on the morning after, she cannot cling to her illusions of safety anymore. Like Juliet, she will need a strategy.

As I say in *The Second Coming of Joan of Arc*, "Rape is the crucifixion of women." Eva, like Joan, rises again from this death. From the limbo of the sanatorium, she resurrects herself with a theatre that she controls. She redeems her pain in roles that tell of women's strength and vindication. She buys out of competing with other women, founding a theatre that aggressively trains and promotes women, enfranchising them economically and fostering their ambitions. She empowers her future lover to support herself financially without a husband, reversing the dynamic that cost her Mimsey's love. And Mimsey, miserable in her marriage, becomes an administrator at the Civic Repertory, standing by Eva as one of her truest friends.

I named the play *Entr'acte*, because the events in women's lives that are expunged from the official records—our rapes and our incest experiences—often provide the turning points in our lives. The "entr'actes" between getting married, giving birth, or achieving mainstream milestones in our careers may constitute our most dramatic and most significant moments, especially for lesbians whose entire lives may be lived in the offstage spaces between the patriarchal acts. This secret three-day stay at the sanatorium was a period of incubation for Eva, who later wrote that she had feared for her sanity. She emerged as a survivor, not a victim, and that is the story I wanted to tell in the play.

The Pele Chant

The original inspiration for *The Pele Chant* was a collection of writings by Haunani-Kay Trask, the leader of the Hawai'ian sovereignty movement. The clarity of her analysis of colonialism was a revelation to me. I was especially interested in her emphasis on the more subtle and insidious process of cultural and spiritual colonization.

The Native culture prior to the landing of Captain Cook was deeply integrated with the beauty and bounty of the land, expressing itself in an economy based on "aloha," or reciprocation. For a nation as large as the U.S., with its history of invasion, occupation, and annexation, an economy like that of pre-colonial Hawai'i without currency, based on exchange without profit, might appear primitive and utopian. For a group of isolated islands, however, pragmatism and ethics would be synonymous.

I was also intrigued by the fact that Native Hawai'ian culture did not have a written language, nor did it have an institution of marriage, the traditional guarantor of paternity in the West. No money, no writing, no marriage…. As a Westerner, it was difficult for me to even conceive of such a culture, because without these three, there can be no ownership, and ownership defines, or at least informs, the majority of relationships in the West. Trask's writings compelled me to look at how notions of fixed ownership permeated every aspect of my thinking. How fluid, how organic a culture without the means for hoarding and monopolizing resources, for splitting the word from its context and depersonalizing it, for owning and exploiting women and children!

I wanted to write about this, but I also wanted to tell the story of Queen Liliuokalani, a Native woman and a person of color, who went up against the interests of white male capitalists and colonizers. Her daughter's history as a "spinster" with a lifelong female companion was intriguing to me as a lesbian, and I was not surprised by the tensions between her and her *hanai* (adoptive) mother.

I was also interested in imagining the dynamics between a white, Western, feminist academic and a Native nonagenarian, both fiercely independent and highly educated. The time of the interview is 1969, an explosive year for liberation movements in this country, and for rising awareness of U.S. imperialism. In a biography of Liliuokalani, I had run across her query, "What did I do that was so wrong as to cause my dear people to lose their country?" This question began to haunt me. Obviously, the deposed Queen was well aware of the extent to which both she and her people had been duped and betrayed. And, still, at the end of her life, she repeatedly asked the question. The quest for an answer became the spine of the play.

The question intrigued me, because, as a survivor, I had expended a great deal of energy and resources studying the ways in which I had been exploited, both as a child and as a woman. I, like Queen Liliuokalani, wondered if there was some way I had contributed to my own oppression. This was a question I could never have asked in early recovery, and to ask it of oneself is not necessarily a prelude to blaming the victim. It can be an attempt to explore the paradigm, which is precisely why the play's Dr. Bateman is so resistant to it. She is powerfully invested in the paradigm that would see Hawai'i and its Queen as helpless victims of a predatory and overwhelming global super-power. In other words, she is deeply invested in the position that it is "too late."

This is the conundrum for the survivor: Healing requires that one come out of denial and accept the fact it is "too late": the loss and violation have occurred, and nothing can ever turn back the clock or make things the same as they were before the trauma. On the other hand, how can one live with any kind of quality when the life sentence of "too late" has been passed? In searching for an answer to the Queen's question, I hoped that I might find some loophole, or some paradigm shift that would allow the survivor/prisoner-of-the-past off the hook.

The story of the priestesses, the *kahunas*, was also in a biography of the Queen, and I found myself returning to it, over and over, because I felt that it held some key to unlocking the past for all colonized people. There seemed to be some secret to this "Pele Chant" that held incredible power, if one could only figure out how to apply it.

Actually, *The Pele Chant* is my own attempt at a "Pele Chant." It was the most laborious writing I have ever done, taking eighteen months for a play that is about twenty-minutes long, consisting of a conversation between two older women seated in chairs. The file for this play is about six-inches thick. I would distill, and then distill again, and then again. The content of the play is like some homeopathic tincture, attenuated so many hundreds of times, I have sometimes wondered if it is not just the essence of the play that remains. And if the homeopathic metaphor holds true, then it should be one of my most effective, healing pieces of writing.

Certainly, this writing deals with the deepest metaphysical inquiry of any of my plays, which, of course, it would have to, because the subject is spiritual colonization. The sympathetic feminist professor is revealed as subscribing to an oppressive colonial paradigm, even as she presses her agenda for liberation. It takes more than recognition of one's status as a victim to liberate oneself, and the ultimate colonization is the colonization of the paradigm of one's thought, which is where the Native, free of written language, has the secret advantage.

The Pele Chant will probably never achieve mainstream popularity in the same way that *The Second Coming of Joan of Arc* has, but the writing of it entailed one of my deepest journeys as a feminist, and it continues to unfold itself to me, as I work to refine my own song of liberation.

Louisa May Incest

As a survivor of sexual abuse, I am always interested in other survivors—especially the ones who write, because writing can be a strategy for survival. One of the interesting things I noted about my own process as a writer was the great difficulty in breaking out of the mold of the patriarchal narrative. There is a kind of powerful, subliminal, gravitational pull that would keep our narratives orbiting like satellites around the interests of this male-dominated planet.

Fortunately for me, I came of age during the explosion of consciousness and activism that characterized the Second Wave of feminism, and this blasted me forever out of that orbit, enabling me and my generation of writers to envision and describe a world in which women are the center and circumference of our own lives.

Women writers of earlier eras have had to forge an uneasy peace between their lived experiences and the myths about women's lives that are perpetuated by a "malestream" culture.

For example, Margaret Mitchell, author of *Gone with the Wind*, was the victim of a brutalizing, attempted marital rape that left her hospitalized and traumatized, sleeping with a gun under her pillow for the rest of her life. How did she gain closure for an assault that society had yet to recognize as a criminal act? She wrote a book in which a marital rape was depicted as the glamorous and romantic climax, after which the rapist completely reformed his life and his victim realized her desire for him. Sadly, a culture of brutalized women eagerly embraced the fantasy.

Louisa May Alcott's *Little Women* has brought to generations of girls one of the most beloved and spunkiest heroines in literature—Jo March. But many of us felt baffled, confused, and betrayed by the final chapters of the book, in which this magnificently independent and spirited girl turns against all of the values for which she has fought so heroically, voluntarily abandoning her cherished dream of becoming a professional writer and surrendering herself to a life of uber-domesticity as the wife of a middle-aged pedant and as a perpetual den mother for a school for little boys. She burns her own writing.

What happened? What could cause an author to so disrupt her own narrative and violate her own alter-ego? The recent biographies of Alcott, as well as the discovery of the pulp fiction she wrote under various pen names, provided me with some clues and inspired the writing of *Louisa May Incest*.

The Rules of the Playground

The Rules of the Playground is a play about the gendered nature of violence, and especially of war. More than that, it is a play about women's denial of this, and our subsequent complicity in the atrocities perpetrated in the name of national security or religious freedom. I wrote it on the eve of the United States' invasion of Iraq.

In the play, the women—all mothers—have come together for a workshop as part of a program sponsored by their children's middle school—a program to eliminate violence in the schools. The program has been designed by so-called experts on global violence. The trainers are analysts from international "think tanks" and peacekeeping organizations. The one thing these pundits never do is analyze or confront acts of war as unacceptable male behaviors. It is my intention to demonstrate that this disguising and protecting of violence as a male prerogative is, in fact, the true agenda behind contemporary, mainstream political analyses.

Thirty years after the Second Wave of women's liberation, we still fail to organize collectively outside of left-wing, male-dominated, ineffectual peace movements, to oppose war as a phenomenon perpetrated by men, serving many of their interests at the expense of women and children. To suggest such a thing is to invite dismissal as a tunnel-visioned, reductionist, somewhat simple-minded holdover from 1970's feminism.

Intelligent women give our precious energy to studying and analyzing the most criminal atrocities as the "natural," "tragic," or "inevitable" results of boundary disputes, ideological conflicts, ethnic and/or religious differences. War is defined in terms of "human nature," never in terms of "male behavior." We are complicit with apparently well-intended efforts of "peacekeepers" to monitor and adjudicate atrocity, in lieu of responding with moral outrage. We buy into the media's categorizing of atrocities committed by "us" as "collateral damages," the result of "necessary targets," and their labeling of atrocities by "them" as acts of terrorism.

In writing *Rules of the* Playground, I looked to Shirley Jackson's unforgettable short story, "The Lottery" for a model. In her story, a ritual atrocity has become "normalized" in the life of a contemporary, small New England town. It is this normalization that is the source of the reader's horror.

In the play, the women have been persuaded that their former approach to playground violence—the use of "timeouts"—is a form of scapegoating that will perpetuate violence. In fact, the "timeout," in which the child is socially isolated for a period of time, is a humane, appropriate, efficient, and effective consequence of indulging in anti-social behavior. Instead of trusting their own judgment, the women are being taught to listen to the experts, and refocus on an obsessive and impossible quest for absolute equality via an ongoing, obsessional remapping of the playground.

The windows are covered, and the mothers are prevented from observing the behaviors of their children on the playground, as this might elicit a too-subjective response to the violence. Women are encouraged by the media to ignore the gendered nature of military violence, adopting male-protectionist analyses that blind us to the true nature and individual motives behind these collective male acts.

In *The Rules of the Playground*, the original women in the workshop are named after famous female political leaders who identified themselves with male-dominated political parties. Shelley, the newcomer, is the only one not so-named, and also the only one to challenge the insanity of the brainwashing that is going on.

I wanted to show the ways in which women train each other to enable male violence through censorship of ourselves, intentional disabling of our powers of observation, and a grotesque enthusiasm for methodologies specifically designed to perpetuate the violence. Conspicuous in its absence is any official and substantive political analysis of the condition of women—a sure indication that women are being recruited to participate in our own oppression.

Finally, I wanted to make the point that it is the women who have experienced the most serious losses who become the self-appointed enforcers of the program. In the play the motives for Jeanne and Madeleine's actions at the end are ambiguous. Certainly, they actively intervene to suppress a potential for resistance, but do they do it in order to justify their own losses, to have the other women experience similar losses, or in some wild hope that the separate space they crave will eventually emerge from an all-out war of mutually assured male destruction?

The women are susceptible to brainwashing, because of their awe of the credentials of the male-identified experts. They are easily shamed about the methods and philosophies they have evolved in the gynocentric field of childcare. They are quick to concur with the trainers that a subjective, emotional response to violence is undesirable, that actual observation of a behavior *as a behavior* is a distraction. But are the women really this gullible? Might it not be that their compliant transfer of focus to the rules of the playground is *their* gendered expression of violence?

Patricide

It is unusual for me to write a play in response to a call for submissions, but the winners of Perishable Theatre's Women Playwrights Festival were invited to submit one-minute plays for a published collection. Challenged by the extreme compression of the format, I wrote *Patricide*.

The cast list describes the only character as "a woman any age, any race, any ethnicity, any size, any sexual orientation, any degree of physical ability." I wanted to make explicit the universality of incest, and also the universality of what I perceive as a survivor's moral imperative to confront perpetrators.

Just as *Entr'acte* is a half-hour condensation of the journey of a survivor from denial to acceptance and integration, *Patricide* is a sixty-second condensation of a survivor's journey from subordination to liberation.

Although, ostensibly, the scene is a dialogue between the woman and her father, it is really a scene between a woman and her terror of the sound of her own voice speaking truth. This is the drama, and this is why the father is not onstage. His responses are not interesting to me. Nothing could be more banal than the rationalizations of a perpetrator. The adult survivor's dialogue with the hypervigilant alter ego she developed as a child is a fascinating drama, because of the depth and complexity of both personalities, as well as the high stakes.

This monologue is actually a teaching model. The woman is terrified, but resolved. She has rehearsed; she is prepared. We hear her say the practiced words, even when her heart is in her mouth. We see her advance, falter, press on—moving mechanically through the recovery script, because in patriarchy, there is no precedent, no social protocol, no opportune moment, no appropriate role model, no archetype or paradigm for a daughter to tell her father what she knows of his criminality, his betrayal, his monstrous selfishness, his exploitation in the attempted soul-murder of his own child.

She has not waited until she was unafraid. She has not waited until he was ready. She has not waited for a supportive or "safe" context, for an opening, for any kind of advantage or leverage, for permission. She has not waited for these, because they will never come.

She knows her situation is paradoxical: The courage she needs for this confrontation will not manifest until *after* she makes the call. She knows he will not accept what she is saying, who she is now. She is not sure who she will be after she makes the call. But she does it anyway.

After her father hangs up on her, she is disoriented, in free-fall. She catches herself by remembering that the call was for her, not him. It was for her, and she did it. And that is a triumph. Yes.

Jane Addams and the Devil Baby

In a collection of writings by Jane Addams, I read about an incident that took place at Hull House in 1912. There was, at that time, a rumor circulating that the settlement house was sheltering a "devil baby," and for weeks, thousands of immigrants had besieged Hull House, demanding to see it. The "devil baby" was, according to an urban legend of the day, an infant born with hooves, horns, and tail as a result of a drunken husband's blasphemous curse that he'd rather see a devil in the house than another baby. Addams placed notices in the paper, attempting to scotch the rumor, but to no avail. Apparently the need to believe that the devil existed in this particular incarnation was deeply embedded in the psyche of these Chicago immigrants, many of whom claimed to know people who had seen a devil baby.

I am intrigued by the meanings behind the stories in the tabloids, and, for this reason, the devil baby phenomenon immediately caught my attention. In the days before suffrage and prohibition, women were at the mercy of their alcoholic husbands, and in a time before legalized, affordable birth control, the timing and frequency of their childbearing was also at the mercy of these men. Abortion, aside from being illegal, was also considered a sin for most of these Italian and Irish Catholic immigrants. When the byproducts of brutal marital rapes would inevitably appear, what a double bind for these poor wives to have to endure the cursing and accusations of the agents of their own oppression! A devil baby would have been an answer to a prayer, in that it would have represented a living reproof to the wicked husband and father who could find it in his heart to curse his own offspring.

I was interested in the historical interface between class and sexual orientation, and in this play I explored how Addams' class privilege had enabled her to live a so-called "spinster's life," with her lesbian partner in a household of philanthropic women. I contrast this with the life of the old Irish immigrant, for whom poverty and compulsory child-bearing had created a vicious cycle of disappointed hopes and tragedy. For women like Kathleen, prayer was their only outlet, and divine intervention their only hope of rescue. Addams did not historically adopt a patronizing attitude toward the superstitious beliefs of immigrants, and I wanted to illustrate her respect for these beliefs, as well as her search for the truth that underlay them.

The play was written during a period in my life when I was confronting my passive conditioning as a middle-class woman and beginning to explore the issue of self-defense. In Kathleen's desperation to see the baby—an indictment of abusive husbands and an absolution for their wives and children—she threatens Jane Addams with a stolen bread knife. She admits later that this is the only time in her life she has used a knife as a weapon. By the end of the play, accepting that there will never be any justice for women and children except that which women themselves demand and enforce, Kathleen admonishes Jane Addams to teach the younger women not to wait for a devil baby, but to be the agents of their own liberation.

Battered on Broadway

Battered on Broadway is subtitled "A Vendetta in One Act," because it is my revenge on the book-writers of the mainstream Broadway musicals who, for decades, have been celebrating the subordination of women— romanticizing dominance and glamorizing sexual violence.

I began with a fantasy of "What if the female lead characters of all the old musicals grew up and got together for some consciousness-raising?" What I eventually settled on was a meeting at Mame's penthouse to discuss the building of a battered women's shelter for the characters in Broadway musicals. The shelter is to be named in honor of Nancy Sykes, the prostituted leading lady who is beaten to death on stage by her boyfriend/pimp in the musical *Oliver!*

I wanted to write a play that allowed the audience to take a second look at these familiar characters, through a contemporary feminist lens. I wanted us to look at the racism, the classism, the misogyny, and the adultism that are so taken for granted in mainstream musicals, and especially in these standards.

But I also wanted to tell a story about middle-class, white feminists who attempt coalition with working-class women and women-of-color. Nellie Forbush DeBecque, army-nurse-turned-plantation-owner, is the organizer of the event. Solidly upper-middle-class, Nellie understands how to use her privilege to influence the media, and she has no intention of letting a grown-up Orphan Annie challenge her leadership of the project, especially when Annie's objection to accepting Daddy Warbucks' contribution would cost them ten million dollars.

I also was interested in the conflicts that arise when oppressed women choose mutually exclusive survival strategies. Aldonza, the successful owner of a brothel, objects when Maria, the Puerto Rican, lesbian separatist, accuses her of collaboration. Maria responds defensively when Aldonza characterizes Maria's poverty as a form of sexual subjugation. The two women drop their feud when Aldonza, expressing sympathy for the onstage, attempted rape of Maria's cousin, reprises the song that was sung in *Man of La Mancha* during her own onstage rape.

The vigilante group in the play is composed of Liza Doolittle, Sally Bowles, and Nancy Sykes (masquerading as Guinevere). Because these are all British characters, and because of Liza's training in impersonation, these seemed like a natural trio to take up the work. Later, I had cause to question my use of white women in these roles. I felt that this disrespected the history of fierce resistance by women of color, but my own choices have been restricted by the fact that I am drawing my characters from those already established by a white mainstream theatre.

Finally, I was also interested in contrasting radical activism which targets the perpetrators with liberal reform that is more focused on providing social services for the victims. The women who are involved in fundraising for the shelter find themselves deferring to Nellie's autocratic style of leadership, for the sake of her access to privilege. Although sympathetic to Annie's tale of incest, they cannot bring themselves to turn down a ten-million-dollar check from her perpetrator. The vigilantes, on the other hand, do not have to make concessions for the sake of expediency. They are not confronted with these kinds of conflicts-of-interest, because they work outside the system. Because of this, they are able to meet Annie's personal need for validation as well as her need for effective action against the perpetrator.

The Obligatory Scene

A One-Act Play for Two Women

Play Summary

Ostensibly arguing about *The Taming of the Shrew,* a lesbian couple come to grips with their own marital struggles and break their deadlock around the issue of sex.

Vivey and Dru are both graduate students, living together in a committed relationship. Vivey's distress over being assigned to direct a scene from *Taming of the Shrew* triggers an argument with her partner about the sexual politics of the play. Dru makes the case that the play is subversive, with Petruchio exaggerating his gender role in order to mock it. Vivey resists this interpretation until Dru cites the dialogue describing the wedding night, where it is apparent that Petruchio does not have sex with Katharine. On the contrary, he delivers a mocking lecture on abstinence.

On the strength of this argument, Vivey accepts that the play might indeed be about a companionate, or even "passing" marriage. She redirects the conversation to address the lack of sex in their own relationship. Dru, a survivor of child sexual abuse, is reluctant to discuss the subject.

As the argument escalates, the two agree to role-play an exercise in which Dru plays an alien from another planet, describing her experience. The exercise, set up to pathologize Dru, backfires on Vivey, and she discovers that she is more accurately the alien from another planet. Dru's experiences are universal and pandemic among women, and Dru's insistence on incorporating that understanding into her practice of intimacy shatters Vivey's complacency and self-righteousness.

Deeply in love, but deeply self-assertive, both women struggle to avoid playing out the traditional "obligatory scene" of a break-up or a sexual stalemate.

The ending of the play points to a radical transformation
the holds the promise of healing for both.

Two females
Forty minutes
Single set

Cast of Characters

<u>Dru</u>: A young woman in her mid-twenties.

<u>Vivey</u>: A young woman in her mid-twenties.

Scene
The bedroom of a small apartment.

Time
The present.

The Obligatory Scene

Setting:

The interior of a bedroom in a small apartment located near a large university. The apartment is inhabited by two lesbian graduate students very different in temperament. There is a double bed and a desk with a computer.

At Rise:

DRU, a young woman in her mid-twenties, lies on the bed, surrounded by books and papers. She has very short hair and is wearing boxer shorts and a sports bra. She is deep into her studies when she hears the offstage arrival of VIVEY.

VIVEY
(Offstage)
I'm going to die! I'm just going to die! I can't believe it!
I just can't believe it! I'm just going to die...
(Hearing VIVEY's voice, DRU quickly rises from the bed, pulls on a tee shirt and a pair of jeans, and crosses to the desk. VIVEY enters.)
I'm going to die!
(DRU does not turn around. VIVEY is a young woman, also in her mid-twenties. She dresses in flamboyant and feminine clothing.)
No...I'm not...I'm not going to die. I'm going to kill him, instead. That's what I'm going to do...I am going

VIVEY (cont'd)

to kill him...
>
> (Pacing as she rants, VIVEY strews her hat,
> scarf, etc. around the apartment.)

Nothing I can do jail-time for, of course. But I *will* have to kill him...I can't believe it. I can't believe what he just did...
>
> (Turning to DRU)

Well, aren't you going to ask?

DRU

I'm going to need more context before I can formulate a meaningful question.

VIVEY

You're going to need more context? Here I am—your partner, your soul-mate, the love of your life—or so you say...I'm *dying*, and you are *going to need more context?* Oh, goddess, whatever possessed me to marry a law school student?

DRU

Are you dying, or are you going to kill someone? I'm confused.
>
> (VIVEY flops on the bed, moaning. DRU sighs.)

Well, I see from the clock that it is 3:45, which, because you insist on setting all the clocks fifteen minutes ahead, actually means it's 3:30. And, because I am wearing my last pair of clean socks, I know it must be Wednesday, because we did laundry last Thursday, and I own just enough pairs to get me through a week. I now have enough information to deduce that you must be returning from your directing class, which is the only afternoon class you have on Wednesdays. This enables me to make a fairly educated guess that the "he" to whom you are referring so pejoratively is the professor

8

DRU (cont'd)

who teaches the directing course, and, because I also
know that you are prone to hyperbole, I can assume that
whatever he did to you is not literally going to cause
your immanent demise—although it might be a
contributing factor to chronic high blood pressure and
possible heart disease down the line, but that, in fact, it
is more likely that your professor has done something
today that has pissed you off. Am I correct?

VIVEY

Pissed me off? No... not "pissed me off." "Pissed me
off" is forgetting my name. "Pissed me off" is standing
me up for an appointment... But, no, "pissed me off" is
not assigning me to direct a scene from the most
woman-hating, the most misogynist, the most male-
supremacist, the most anti-feminist, the most
heterosexist, the most *disgusting* play in the world! No,
he did not "piss me off." He is trying to destroy my soul.

DRU

Ah.

VIVEY
(Turning over on the bed to face DRU)
Well?

DRU

Well?

VIVEY
Don't you want to know what the play is? Or do you
still need more "context?"

DRU

What's the play?

VIVEY

Taming of the Shrew.

DRU

Ah.

VIVEY

Taming of the Shrew... William Shakespeare...Surely somewhere in your pre-law, minimally-required, English lit classes you must have encountered it...?

DRU

Mmmm...

VIVEY

Taming of the "SHREW?" Elizabethan for "bitch...?"

DRU

Got it.

VIVEY

He assigned me to direct it, because he knows I'm a dyke. He did it on purpose. This is classic harassment.
    (She turns and looks at DRU.)
Well?
    (DRU shrugs.)
Is that all you have to say?
    (She imitates the shrug.)

DRU

I like the play.

VIVEY

You *like* the play? No. This is a joke. You *like Taming of the Shrew*?

DRU

I do.

VIVEY

Don't you think that's taking the "female masculinity" thing a little too far?

DRU

It's a very radical play.

VIVEY

Oh, right!

DRU

It's subversive.

VIVEY

No, it's not. There's nothing subversive about emotional abuse.

DRU

What if it's not?

VIVEY

He puts food in front of her that he won't let her eat, he shows her presents that he won't let her have, he humiliates her in front of her family...

DRU

I remember a story about a Confederate prison guard during the Civil War—

VIVEY

Is this going to have anything to do with what we're talking about?

DRU

This guard would always single out one of the prisoners-of-war for abuse. He would make the guy's life hell, and then one day, the guard would walk into the prison and order the prisoner to follow him. He would say he had a special work detail for him. And, of course, the other prisoners were sure he was going to murder the guy. So, the guard takes the guy and shows him into his office. Then he closes the door and leaves him there, with a suit of civilian clothes draped over the back of a chair and a set of keys on the table.

VIVEY

So?

DRU

The guard never said a kind word to the prisoner. He never let on he was a Union sympathizer. He acted like an enemy the whole time. But the prisoner, if he had any brains, would figure out it had all been a game to help him escape. The way the system was, the game was the only way the guard could show support without getting both of them killed.

VIVEY

Oh, that is totally not what is going on in *Taming*! Petruchio is a complete misogynist, and he means what he says.

DRU

And what does he say?

VIVEY

Well, it just so happens that I have it here. It's actually part of the scene I have been assigned to direct.
> (She pulls out a paperback edition of the play and opens it to a bookmark..)

VIVEY (cont'd)

"I will be master of what is mine own./ She is my
goods, my chattels; she is my house,/ My household
stuff, my field, my barn/ My horse, my ox, my ass, my
anything…"
    (She closes the book.)
Case closed.

DRU

Let me see…
    (She takes the book.)

VIVEY

I didn't make it up.

DRU

I know. I just want to get a little context here.

VIVEY

Context!

DRU
    (Reading)
"This mad-brain'd bridegroom took him such a cuff/
That down fell the priest and book and book and
priest…"
    (VIVEY starts to interrupt.)
Wait!
    (Reading again)
"He calls for wine: 'A health!' quoth he…And threw the
sops all in the sexton's face…"
    (Looking up)
So he decks the priest and heaves his drink in the
sexton's face.

VIVEY

He's a pig.

DRU

But even a pig knows the farmer that feeds him.

VIVEY

Meaning?

DRU

Meaning that if Petruchio was all that keen on owning a woman, one would expect that he would show a little more respect for the Church and the ceremony that legitimize that ownership.

VIVEY

He doesn't think that far. He's just a jerk.

DRU

I don't agree. The men who really want to control women are the biggest romantics in the world. They would never come out and name what they're doing the way Petruchio does. And the reason he *can* name it is because he's not playing that game. He doesn't want to own Katharine. He wants to free her.

VIVEY

But he just married her.

DRU

To save her! She was being hideously abused by her father. She was a prisoner in his house. Nobody loved her there.

VIVEY

At least they fed her.

DRU

But don't you see? That was his point in denying her
food and clothes. He was refusing to participate in the
traditional prostituted exchange of goods for sex that
was implicit in Elizabethan marriage.

VIVEY

So he was going to liberate her by starving her?

DRU

He was trying to get her to shift paradigms.

VIVEY

Why am I arguing with you? You're a lawyer. You
could defend Jack the Ripper.
     (She begins thumbing through the script.)

DRU

Actually, I would have taken a shot at the insanity plea.
It seems that the fellow who was the Ripper was a
victim of torture as a child. He was born intersex and
had three operations performed on his genitals before he
was even five—operations without anaesthetics, no
sterile procedures—

VIVEY

    (Looking up)
Okay, if Petruchio is all about liberating her, why does
he order Katharine around like a servant in front of her
family at the end of the play?

DRU

It's the game. She's finally figured it out, and she's
playing it with him.

15

VIVEY

What game?

DRU

The dominance game...like the prison guard. She was "fucking with gender."

VIVEY

Oh, yeah, pretending to obey your husband is really going to fuck with gender.

DRU

Okay, if the play is really about breaking a woman's spirit, then why doesn't Petruchio rape her on the wedding night?

VIVEY

He probably does.

DRU

No, he doesn't.

VIVEY

How do you know? They don't show the wedding night.

DRU

No, but they describe it.

VIVEY

Where?

DRU

(Finding it)
"Grumio: Where is he?
Curtis: In her chamber, making a sermon of continency to her."

16

VIVEY

Where? Let me see…
(Reading)
"And rails and swears and rates, that she poor
soul,/ Knows not which way to stand, to look, to
speak…"
(Looking up)
See? He's verbally abusing her.

DRU

(Reading)
"And sits as one new-risen from a dream."
(Looking up)
"As one new-risen from a dream."

VIVEY

Yeah. Battered-woman syndrome.

DRU

No…Shifting into another the paradigm.

VIVEY

No.

DRU

She's been expecting he's going to rape her, which, of
course, he would do—and the sooner the better, if it's all
about domination. But instead he takes her up to the
bedroom and gives her this mock lecture on abstinence.
He doesn't touch her. He's not going to touch her. Now
she is completely confused. Isn't that the whole point of
marriage? So, he's going to keep her hungry and he's
not going to let her sleep, and these are classic
brainwashing techniques—except that she's already
been brainwashed by the patriarchy and he's trying to
un-brainwash her…

17

VIVEY

You know, you have a point...Why wouldn't he rape
her?

DRU

And why would the playwright go to such pains to let us
know that he doesn't?

VIVEY

Well, he doesn't really go to "such pains." If your theory
holds, then this is really the obligatory scene, and he
doesn't show it.

DRU

The obligatory scene?

VIVEY

The scene that provides the key to understanding the
whole play. And he doesn't show it. In fact, it's just a
couple of lines between two servants. Easy to cut. If
Shakespeare was all that great of a playwright, he would
have given us the scene.

DRU

But that's just exactly his point. He couldn't.

VIVEY

Why not?

DRU

Because he knew his audience would not be able to
accept it, just like Petruchio knew that his social peers
were not going to accept an egalitarian, companionate
marriage. It was the sixteenth century...

VIVEY

Oh, and women enjoyed being raped by their husbands
back then?

DRU

No, but they had no choice. Shakespeare knew what he
could get away with and what he couldn't. If he had
staged that scene, it wouldn't have made sense to
anybody, except maybe the gay men who were in
passing marriages.

VIVEY

(Sarcastically)
Like himself?

DRU

(Shrugging)
The case could be made.

VIVEY

Okay.
　　　(A long pause. VIVEY watches DRU. DRU
　　　turns back to her books.)
And what about us?

DRU

What do you mean?

VIVEY

Our passing marriage.

DRU

But we're both out.

VIVEY

But we don't have sex.

19

DRU

Yes, we do.
(VIVEY gives her a look.)
All you have to do is ask.

VIVEY

What about *you*? You *never* ask.

DRU

Because it's not the same for me, Vivey. I don't like it as much as you do.

VIVEY

You don't like it at all.

DRU

I'm just not a very sexual person.
(Turning away from VIVEY)
Why are we having this conversation? You know that.

VIVEY

So why *do* you have sex with me?

DRU

Because it seems to be such a big deal to you.

VIVEY

Well, how do you think that makes me feel?

DRU

I don't know, Vivey. I'm not you.

VIVEY

This is interrupting your work, isn't it?

DRU

Yes, but it's all right.

VIVEY

Could you just *try*?

DRU

Vivey—

VIVEY

I want to make love to you. Not every night...just
sometimes.

DRU
(Angry, DRU turns to face her.)
Why? You know I don't like it.

VIVEY

Because that's what lovers do!

DRU

How do you know? How do you know what other
lesbians do? Have you asked them? Do you think
they're going to tell you if they're not having sex? I
don't tell people. Maybe you do—

VIVEY

No, I don't.

DRU

Well, then don't go around making assumptions about
what other people do in bed...
(A pause)
Look, Vivey...it's biochemical. It has nothing to do with
how I feel about you. It's brain chemistry.

VIVEY

Oh, so I'm just some kind of endorphin junkie, because I like sex.

DRU

Well, something like that. It's dopamine and norepinephrine. People who are in love have higher levels of them in the brain—and that triggers production of testosterone, which is the chemical that makes both men and women get horny.

VIVEY

That is *so* unromantic!

DRU

But it's true! We're animals, and all that chemistry is about procreating and preserving the gene pool. It doesn't have anything to do with dykes.

VIVEY

Except that dykes are dykes because we feel sexual desire for other women.

DRU

Okay.

VIVEY

And maybe I do desire you because on some primitive level your strong little body and your massive little brain seem worthy of passing on, but the fact is I do desire you, and I want to touch you, and excite you, and I want to see you have this *huge* orgasm in my arms...

DRU

(Embarrassed)

Vivey—

22

VIVEY

…Screaming and throwing your head back and
thrashing around and for once in your life letting me
have the control.

DRU

Okay, fine. An orgasm like you? Okay.
(She crosses to the bed and does her impression
of VIVEY's orgasms.)

VIVEY

(Shocked)
That's what I look like?

DRU

(Angry)
Yeah.

VIVEY

I'm never going to have sex with you again.

DRU

Vivey—

VIVEY

That was just cruel, Dru. And unnecessary. Just because
you're self-conscious about your sexuality, you have no
right to make other people ashamed of theirs.
(She starts to exit.)

DRU

I'm sorry, Vivey...I thought...I'm sorry! Please—
(Shaking her head, VIVEY doesn't turn.)
Vivey, please...Show me what *I* look like.
(VIVEY turns.)
Show me what *I'm* like in bed.

DRU (cont'd)
(VIVEY looks at DRU.)
Really.

VIVEY

I wouldn't be that unkind.

DRU

No. I want to know.
(She invites her to the bed.)

VIVEY

I can show you right here. I don't need a bed. I don't
even need a real person.
(With a bored expression, she takes the doorknob
in her hand and rattles it back and forth. She
speaks to the door.)
"No, I'm fine. I can keep going."

DRU

(Horrified)
No.

VIVEY

Yes.

DRU

That must feel terrible.

VIVEY

No, actually, I don't let it. I close my eyes and imagine
you really enjoying it, and me being able to make love
to you, and then, yes, with my eyes closed, I have those
terrific orgasms that you think are so funny. Because I
don't want to let you know how bad you are.

DRU

Well...
        (A long pause)
I guess we're even.

VIVEY

I guess we are. Who's going to sleep in the living room?

DRU

Who's going to move out?
        (VIVEY doesn't say anything. She sits.)
Vivey, I can't be someone I'm not.

VIVEY

But you used to be.

DRU

When?

VIVEY

When we first got together. We were having sex all the
time. Don't you remember?

DRU

        (Uncomfortable)
I remember...But it's like the way someone remembers
what they did when they were drunk.

VIVEY

But we weren't drinking...

DRU

The dopamine...
        (VIVEY makes a sound of exasperation.)
It's true! It's like a drug! They can inject it into prairie
dogs—

VIVEY

I don't want to talk about prairie dogs! And I don't want
to talk about monkeys, or dolphins or whales or
anything else! I want to talk about us!

DRU

(Angry)
That's what I *am* talking about. I'm talking about us as
animals. We aren't mystical beings who met in some
past life…

VIVEY

All right, animals. Let's talk about the *conditioning* that
happens to animals when they're young—

DRU

(A warning)
I'm not going there.

VIVEY

Why not?

DRU

You know why… I've done the therapy, I've done the
groups, I've read the books, I've written the journals,
I've beaten the pillows, and I'm done. I told you that
when we met. I'm not doing any more work around the
sexual abuse.

VIVEY

But that's what this is about… It's not natural not to
want sex.

DRU

And I think it's not natural to want it all the time.

VIVEY

I don't want it *all* the time.

DRU

And you know what . . .? You want to talk about
conditioning? You get all turned on by the sight of me in
boxer shorts. You get all turned on when I wear a jacket
with a tie. You get all turned on when I get a haircut.
That shit's not about me. It's not about who I am. It's a
piece of theatre.

VIVEY

Yeah, well, you used to get turned on by my lingerie,
and I didn't mind. I liked it. I wish you would now.

DRU

Vivey, did it ever occur to you that my not wanting sex
with you is *healthy*? That this is what *my* healing looks
like? That, because I was abused as a child, I have had
to go all the way to the roots of what sex is in a way that
other people might not, and that I am not comfortable
with those dopamine highs or conditioned responses to
women's underwear anymore? Did it ever occur to you
that I am really loving you, not just "in love" anymore?

VIVEY

And what does that make me? Some kind of emotionally
stunted primitive?

DRU

It doesn't make you anything. I was talking about me.

VIVEY

I like sex.

27

DRU

I'm not arguing with that. I know you like sex, and I don't.

VIVEY

You don't even like touching me, do you?

DRU

I love touching you. I don't do it, because you always get turned on. And then I feel like I'm expected to perform.

VIVEY
(Turning away with a sigh)
What would Shakespeare do?

DRU

Probably go find a boy.

VIVEY
(Turning back to DRU)
What if we *did* exaggerate the difference...the way Petruchio does?

DRU

It would be tough to exaggerate.

VIVEY

What do you mean?

DRU

We already come from two different worlds.

VIVEY
(A pause)
That's it...
(Another pause)

28

VIVEY (cont'd)
That's it..."We come from two different worlds..."
>	(She takes one of her shopping bags and begins
>	to rip two holes in it.)

DRU
Oh, no…

VIVEY
Come on...It'll be fun. You can *literally* come from a
different world...A different *planet*...

DRU
I'm not an actor.

VIVEY
>	(Finishing up the bag)
Oh, come on...You're going to be a lawyer.

DRU
Meaning I should be able to act, or that I'm an alien life
form?

VIVEY
Both. Here... We'll just put this on you...and, voilá!
>	(She puts the bag over DRU's head.)

DRU
I feel like an idiot.

VIVEY
Everyone from your planet looks like this.

DRU
What about you?

VIVEY

I'm from Earth. Can you see?

DRU

No, but where I come from, we all have extra-sensory
perception.

VIVEY

Okay…I'll just go out in the hall, and you go in the
bathroom, and then we'll meet...
(VIVEY starts to exit.)

DRU

Wait! How are we going to understand each other?

VIVEY

(She grabs DRU's computer headset and puts it
on.)
Simultaneous translation.

DRU

What about me?

VIVEY

ESP, remember?
(She exits. DRU tries to exit for the bathroom
and runs into a wall. She finally exits. The stage
is empty for a moment. VIVEY enters.)
Dru? Dru?

DRU/ ALIEN

(From the bathroom, speaking in a monosyllabic,
monotone)
What is "Dru?"

VIVEY

Oh…
(DRU enters with a bath towel for a cape.)
Love the bath towel…

DRU/ ALIEN

What is "bath to-wel?"

VIVEY

Right.

DRU/ ALIEN

Gree-tings.

VIVEY

Greetings.
(After an awkward pause)
Chair?

DRU/ ALIEN

What is "chair?"
(DRU sits on the desk.)

VIVEY

Okay… Well…So we are here today to tell each other
about our bodies—

DRU/ ALIEN

No!
(VIVEY looks surprised.)
I did not come here to talk about the bo-dy.

VIVEY

(Confused)
But, Dru…

DRU/ ALIEN

What is "Dru?"

VIVEY

(Annoyed)
I thought this was the whole point…

DRU/ ALIEN

We do not have bo-dies an-y-more. They were co-lo-nized, and so we had to a-ban-don them. We dis-trust you. We dis-trust your mo-tives.

VIVEY

(Sitting)
Oh.

DRU/ ALIEN

Good-bye.
        (She starts to cross to the bathroom.)

VIVEY

Wait! I'm sorry. On my planet, everybody has a body.

DRU/ ALIEN

That is not true on my pla-net.

VIVEY

Okay, but what if I want to talk about *my* body?

DRU/ ALIEN

(Making a ear-splitting, audio-feedback noise)
Eeee-ee-eee!
        (She grabs her head.)
War-ning! War-ning! This is a trap! This is a trap!

VIVEY

Dru!

DRU/ ALIEN

What is "Dru?"

VIVEY
(Exasperated, she pulls off the headset.)
We can't communicate at all!

DRU
(Coming out of character)
I thought that was understood.
(VIVEY looks at her for a moment. She
resumes the game.)

VIVEY

Okay. My people want to give you *gifts*... We came here
to tell you about the *gifts* we give on my planet.

DRU/ ALIEN

That is some-thing we can talk about. We can-not talk
about bo-dies.

VIVEY
(After a long pause)
Alright.
(Uncomfortable)
You better go first.

DRU/ ALIEN

My peo-ple had bo-dies. They were wi-red to our brains.
The peo-ple who gave us the bo-dies were sup-posed to
pro-gram us so that our bo-dies and our brains would
work to-ge-ther for our be-ne-fit. But our cre-a-tors were
e-vil. They pro-grammed us for their own use in-stead.

DRU/ ALIEN (cont'd)

They co-lo-nized our bo-dies and then they pro-
grammed our brains to be-lieve this was our pur-pose,
that this was good, that we liked it—that this was good,
that we liked it. We are pro-grammed to self-des-truct
an-y time we be-gan to sus-pect the truth of our con-di-
tion—the truth of our con-di-tion—the truth of our con-
di-tion. Man-y of us die. Man-y of us re-main slaves.
Those of us who ma-nage to de-pro-gram our-selves become ver-y un-sta-ble in the pro-cess. Not all of us can
de-pro-gram—not all of us. The co-lo-ni-zers are still in
con-trol of our pla-net and those of us who have de-pro-
grammed our-selves must hide all the time. We must
pre-tend we are still co-lo-nized. We can-not tell who is
safe—who is safe—and who is not. We are in dan-ger
from the co-lo-ni-zers and al-so from the hid-den self-
des-truct files that are still in our brains. We have had to
dis-a-ble all con-nec-tions to the bo-dy. O-ther-wise, the
vo-lume of con-tra-dic-to-ry mes-sa-ges could o-ver-
whelm the sys-tem and cause it to shut down—to shut
down—to shut down...

> (Moved, VIVEY takes a step toward DRU. DRU
> responds with the feedback noise again.)

Eeee-ee-eee!

> (VIVEY stops.)

Do not touch me! Do not touch me!

VIVEY

> (Backing away)

Okay!

> (A pause. VIVEY is hurt and angry.)

I'm sorry about what happened to you. I'm sorry about
your people...And I'm sorry you're having to live in
hiding. It would almost be easier to stay colonized.

DRU/ ALIEN

No. That is li-ving death.

VIVEY

Are you afraid now?

DRU/ ALIEN

We are a-fraid all the time. You have no word—no word—no word in your lan-guage for the le-vel of fear that is our de-fault. But some of us can func-tion ver-y well, be-cause of this fear. E-ve-ry-thing else is eas-y com-pared with this. E-ve-ry-thing else is ea-sy—e-ve-ry-thing else is ea-sy...

VIVEY

I'm so sorry.
        (A long silence)

DRU/ ALIEN

Tell us about your peo-ple.

VIVEY

Well...We have not been colonized, and so we have a very different relationship to the b-word we're not supposed to talk about. We like to touch our own b-word, and we like to have other people touch them, and this is how we show our love for—

DRU/ ALIEN

        (Feedback screech)
Eeee-ee-eee! War-ning! Dan-ger!

VIVEY

But I don't come from your planet!

DRU/ ALIEN

How do I know you are not one of them?

VIVEY

(Exasperated)
You'll just have to trust me!

DRU/ ALIEN

(Covering her ears, DRU backs away,
screaming.)
Eeee-ee-eee! No...No! No!

VIVEY

(Angry)
Then *don't* trust me! I don't care! I'm just *visiting*!
(DRU continues to withdraw.)
Oh, for chrissake...I'm not going to hurt you!
(DRU curls into a fetal position.)
What?

DRU/ALIEN

(Panting, she recites:)
"I'm not go-ing to hurt you!" "I'm not go-ing to hurt
you!" "I'm not go-ing to hurt you!"

VIVEY

But I'm *not*—
(Suddenly DRU becomes motionless, catatonic.)
I can't say anything, can I? Dru...? Dru...?
(VIVEY crosses to her and rips the bag off her
head.)
Stop it! You're scaring me!

DRU

(As herself)
You're the one scaring me!

VIVEY

I don't like this game.
> (VIVEY sits on the bed. There is a moment of
> tense silence. Both women are angry.)

DRU

You want to know why you don't like it?

VIVEY

Because you were screaming at me.

DRU

No. Because it wasn't about you. It was about me. You
couldn't stand that.

VIVEY

That's not true.

DRU

They why don't you put the bag on your head and be the
alien, and *I'll* be the normal one?

VIVEY

But you're *not* normal!

DRU

> (Exasperated)

Vivey, I'm more normal than you are! Turn on the TV,
turn on the radio, log on to the Internet! Read a fucking
newspaper, sometime, why don't you? Any
newspaper—any page—any day! Women are colonized
globally...one out of three girls raped, one out of four
women battered...prostitution, pornography, trafficking,
incest, harassment, genital mutilation...what? We do
ninety percent of the work on the planet and own less
than ten percent of the property!

DRU (cont'd)
(She grabs a stack of newspaper from her desk.)
This, this *right here* IS my planet.
(She throws the stack on the bed.)
I'm not the one with my head in a fucking bag!
(There is a long silence.)

VIVEY
(Quietly)
I don't let it get to me. The one thing I *can* own is my sexuality.

DRU
You *own* it, because you *bought* it. But who sold it to you—and *why*?

VIVEY
(A long pause)
Okay...let's say *I'm* the alien.
(DRU crosses to her and begins to put the bag on VIVEY's head. Suddenly, VIVEY panics.)
No...no! Don't! Stop it! Don't! Stop it!
(She and DRU wrestle for the bag. VIVEY rips it up.)
I don't want to see things the way you do! I don't want to be like you!
(She begins to tear the bag into pieces.)

DRU
(Watching her)
So you *do* know.

VIVEY
Yes, of course, I do...I'm not stupid.
(DRU gets up and crosses slowly to the door.)
Don't go.

DRU
(DRU turns and faces her in silence for a
moment.)
It's really dangerous for me to stay.

VIVEY
I can't live like you. I can't let it control my life the way
it controls yours.

DRU
And I can't let your denial control me anymore.
(Stricken, VIVEY says nothing.)
I really have to go.
(She crosses to the door.)
I'll come back and get my stuff tomorrow when you're
in class.
(She exits. VIVEY, numb, begins to pick up the
pieces of the shredded bag. After a moment,
DRU re-enters.)
I need to take my books. Test tomorrow.
(She crosses to her desk and begins to collect her
books.)

VIVEY
(Watching her, VIVEY begins to formulate a
plan.)
Dru...
(DRU turns.)
Please...couldn't we just separate from...
(DRU looks at her.
...from...all that...that . . .
(VIVEY indicates the newspapers on the bed.)

DRU
Context?

DRU (cont'd)
(VIVEY looks down. DRU responds with
gentleness.)
That's how it works, Vivey. That's how people get
colonized. They learn to separate the roles they play
from the social context that dictates them. They
persuade themselves that they have chosen the roles.
That's colonization.

VIVEY
But look at Petruchio—He saw the roles, he knew the
context—but he didn't buy into it. *He* found another
way—

DRU
He found another way because he wasn't interested in
having sex with Katharine. He was already outside the
central paradigm of patriarchy—

VIVEY
Well, all right. Maybe he *was* gay, but I don't think you
should walk out on me. I think that's just the flip side of
sexual pressure.

DRU
No! That's the old "reverse discrimination" argument.
There is so much pressure to have sex in this culture, it's
nauseating. You have the weight of the entire culture on
your side, Vivey. It's not a fair fight. I'm pretty isolated
in my perspective.

VIVEY
You're my *world,* Dru. Your perspective is a huge
chunk of my context.
(A pause)
What if I did join you on your planet.

40

DRU

(Angry)
This planet!

VIVEY

This planet. If I gave up everything I know about sex,
would you trust me enough to try to reinvent it?
(Pause)
I know... "Sounds like a trap..."

DRU

Well, it does.

VIVEY

I think it's a trap for you to leave me. I think walking
out on someone who loves you is just about the most
robot, colonial, bullshit thing you can do. Maybe love is
a whole other circuitry. Maybe it doesn't require any of
the wires you had to disconnect. Maybe it's something
beyond both our wildest dreams, but we're never going
to know if you leave.
(She crosses to her dresser.)
Here... Here!
(She starts pulling out all her lingerie and
throwing it on the floor.)
Here's all those bras, and those panties, and those
teddies—and everything... Take them. Take the makeup.
Take the hair doo-dads...Take everything!
(She tears apart her bureau and sweeps clean the
top of it.)

DRU

Vivey...
(Concerned, she sets down her books.)

VIVEY

(Angry)

No, it's true. They have a context. Of course, they have a context. That's why I wear them. Now, here's my question—Do you *really* want me without them? Do you want me if I'm not being the femme who pines after her unavailable partner? Do you really want me as a hairless primate who is dead serious about loving you? Called your bluff, didn't I? Let's see you drop the stone butch for me!

DRU

(Struggling)

I can't.

VIVEY

Then let's be clear about who is more colonized.

DRU

I can't believe you would—

VIVEY

Well, try me. Damn it, Dru—Let's just *try*!

DRU

(After a long pause)

I don't know how.

VIVEY

Well, I don't either.
(They look at each other.)

DRU

(Slowly)

Actually...I think this is a very promising start.
(VIVEY looks at her. DRU smiles.)

VIVEY
(Smiling back)
So do I.

(BLACKOUT)

THE END

Bite My Thumb

A Skirmish in One Act

For Pat Schmatz

For the courage and integrity of her life
and her generosity in sharing the story of it with me.

Play Summary

Two "gangs" from rival Off-Off Broadway productions of *Romeo and Juliet* meet in an alley to rumble, sixteenth-century style. Female-to-male transgender meets lesbian cross-dressing, and lesbian butch squares off against male machismo in this swashbuckling gender-bender!

A male "Romeo" from a traditional production shows up at the stage door of an all-women theatre company, challenging their "Romeo" to come out and fight like a man. The fact that this cross-dressing, female Romeo has stolen his former girlfriend by offering her the role of Juliet only fans the flames of his indignation. When Juliet's nurse, a lesbian butch, takes up his challenge, however, Romeo finds himself outclassed in the martial arts. On the brink of surrender, he is rescued by his own masked "Mercutio," who takes on the Nurse in a dazzling display of sword-fighting techniques.

In another surprise twist, "Mercutio" is unmasked, revealing his identity as a transgendered male. Accused of being a woman by his former buddy, he is also attacked by the lesbian butch for alleged lesbo-phobia. Meanwhile, the female "Romeo," threatened by the butch's superior fighting skills attempts to put her back in her place as a character actor. The butch, however, joins forces with the transgender actor, with the result that both find themselves expelled from their respective companies.

Having pronounced a plague on both their houses, the butch launches into a tender coda about the unsung heroism of those who renounce gender roles, the female Cyrano's whose stories will never make the stages of mainstream theatre. She discards her skirt, as the erstwhile Mercutio detaches his codpiece, and the two

49

warriors exit the stage committed to creating a new kind of theatre that can support their stories.

Two males, four females
Thirty minutes
Single set

Cast of Characters

<u>Joe</u>: A traditionally handsome young man in his early twenties.

<u>Ben</u>: Romeo's sidekick, a stout young man in his early twenties.

<u>Mark</u>: A new member of Romeo's company, young, twenty-something.

<u>Julie:</u> A traditionally beautiful young woman in her early twenties.

<u>Jo</u>: A large, older, butch lesbian.

<u>Roz:</u> Juliet's lover, the head of an all-women Shakespeare company, an alpha femme.

Scene

An alley outside the stage door of an Off-Off Broadway theatre.

Time

The present.

Bite My Thumb

Setting: An alley in New York City, just outside the stage door of an Off-Off Broadway theatre. There is a dumpster, with several trashcans, outside the door. Depending on the ambitiousness of the stage-fighting choreography, there can be a variety of objects, pallets, etc., which would lend themselves to creative weaponry and various playing levels.

At Rise: Three figures enter furtively. They are dressed in male period costumes from an Off-Off Broadway production of *Romeo and Juliet*. JOE, who is dressed as Romeo, has the traditional male-model looks of a romantic lead. His sidekick BEN, dressed as Benvolio, is stockier, a traditional supporting actor. MARK, dressed as Mercutio, is skinny and masked. All three carry the swords that are a part of their costumes. JOE advances aggressively toward the state door, MARK in tow. BEN tries to block them.

BEN
(Blocking JOE)
Come on, man! We can't be screwing around like this! We've got a show to do!

JOE

(Continuing to advance)
Get out of my way, Ben. I don't want to have to hurt you.

BEN

What's up with that, "I don't want to hurt you?"

JOE

I'm serious, Ben. Get out of my way.

BEN

(To MARK)
Mark, man, what are you doing? You don't want to encourage him, do you?

MARK

This is men's business.

BEN

"Men's" business? Have you both lost your minds? What about "actors'" business? Joe, you're playing Romeo in forty-five minutes, and Mark—dude—you're playing Mercutio. We don't have time for this shit!

JOE

(Advancing)
Then think of it as a little pre-show warm-up.

BEN

Warm-up? Man, what if they kick your butts?

JOE

(Turning)
Ben, they're *girls.*

BEN

So?

JOE

So you really think they're going to kick our butts?
(MARK sniggers.)

BEN

(Serious)
Yeah, they could kick your butts. How long have you
two been taking stage-fighting classes?

JOE

That's not the point.

MARK

Yeah!

BEN

That is *totally* the point. You don't know what the hell
you're doing!

JOE

Do you want me to prove it?
(Drawing a sword)

BEN

Oh, man, I can't believe this shit!

JOE

Scared?

BEN

Come on, this is me, Ben—your best friend. Me, Ben.
You, Joe. We're in New York City, Lower East Side.
Yo—this isn't Verona. We're in a *play*. And it sure isn't

55

BEN (cont'd)
West Side Story, with a bunch of guys running around in
tights.

JOE
Ben, you don't understand. This is war.

BEN
No, no... War is when big metal things drop out of the
sky and explode, knocking down buildings and killing
people. It's not when an underemployed actor goes
looking to have a duel with his ex-girlfriend's new
lover.

JOE
War is when you have an enemy, and we have an
enemy.

BEN
No, we don't. We have *competition*.

JOE
　　(Exploding)
Competition! Do you think it's a coincidence that there
happens to be another production of *Romeo and Juliet* at
exactly the same time as our production?

BEN
Hello? This is New York City... Happens all the time.

JOE
No, it doesn't happen all the time, because *this*
production is an all-female one, and *their* Juliet happens
to have been *my* Juliet, and *their* Romeo just happens to
be her new girlfriend, and *this* is an act of war.

BEN

(Turning to MARK)
Right?

MARK

Right!

BEN

You're just going to make a fool of yourself.

JOE

No, you're the one making a fool of yourself, letting
these dykes steal our box office and pretend they've got
a better show than ours, when all they are is a bunch of
freaks, and all they've got is a *freak* show, and that's
what people are paying to see: a bunch of drag kings
with socks in their codpieces, running around pretending
they're us. They want to be men, fine. Let 'em come out
here and fight us like men.

MARK

Yeah!

BEN

You're just pissed because your girlfriend left you for a
woman.

JOE

(Enraged)
No! No, she did *not!* She left me for a part! She left me
because she was an understudy in my company, and that
wasn't good enough for her. She left me for someone
who would let her play Juliet, and that someone just
happens to be a woman. But she's no more lesbian than
Mark.

MARK

Hey! I'm not a lesbian!

JOE

Chill. I'm making a point here.

BEN

You are going to look like the biggest sexist jerk…

JOE

Sexist? You want to know who's sexist? Women who can't figure out any better way to get an audience than to dress up like men, take a great classic play, and turn it into some kind of a joke. Why don't they do a woman's play? If they're so feminist, why don't they do that?

BEN

In the first place, there aren't any classic women's plays…

JOE

Exactly—

BEN

And in the second place, maybe because they want to fight.

JOE

(Turning toward the stage door)
Yeah, well, bring it on!
                    BEN

I mean on stage.

JOE

They want to play men, let them come out here and fight like men.

58

BEN

Dude, we're *actors*. We can't fight any better than they can.

JOE

We'll see about that!

BEN

Oh, come on! We've had two weeks of stagefighting lessons.

JOE

Wrong! Wrong! Did they ever grow up as guys? Did they ever get teased for backing down? Did they ever get humiliated for running away from a fight? Did anyone ever tell them they couldn't cry? Did they grow up knowing if there ever was going to be a draft, they'd have to go out and kill people? So maybe we don't have all that much time in with the fencing, but we've grown up fighting! They can't just strap on a sword— or anything else—and pretend to be us. No way! They want the privilege that comes with being men, then they're going to have to prove themselves, just like we have to every day of our lives! And I'll tell you something else—You want to talk "sexist?"—what about a director who casts her new girlfriend in the lead role? What about that? Isn't that sexual harassment, or something?

BEN

Maybe she thought Julie was a good actor.

JOE

Oh, come on, Ben.

BEN

I think you intimidated her…

JOE

Intimidated her? Oh, come on? How did I do that?
    (Backing BEN into a wall)
Tell me, man! How did I intimidate Julie?

BEN

Like this.

JOE

Oh, man...I can't argue with you. You want to go back,
fine, but me and "Mercutio" here, we're going to kick
some feminist butt.

BEN

    (to MARK)
You're not going to encourage him, are you? And
what's with the mask?

MARK

I'm practicing. I have to fight with a mask in the play.

BEN

Oh, right…
    (While BEN has been talking to MARK, JOE
    has gone up to the stage door. He is banging on
    it.)
No...man! Don't do that—!
JOE

    (Turning)
Hey! You don't want to be here, you can leave—

             Just then, the door opens,
             slamming JOE in the face

and knocking him off the
stoop. JULIE stands in the
doorway, framed in light.
She is dressed as Juliet
and looks as lovely as one
would expect.

JULIE
(Looking at MARK)
Who are you? What do you want?

JOE
(Stepping out from behind the door)
Well, if it isn't the East and Juliet the sun…

JULIE
Oh, God…
(JULIE slams the door.)

BEN
I told you, man.

JOE
You didn't tell me anything.
(He begins to bang on the door. There is no
response, and he bangs more aggressively.)
BEN
Come on...
(JOE persists in banging. JULIE opens the door
again.)

JULIE
Go away!

JOE
No!

JULIE

I have a show!

JOE

So do I.
>   (She tries to close the door, but he sticks his
>   sword in it.)
Hey! Don't break my sword!

JULIE

Then get it out of the door!

JOE

I just wanted to talk.

JULIE

It's over, Joe! Get it? Now, leave me alone...
>   (To BEN)
Ben, tell him to leave me alone.

JOE

What makes you think I'm here to see you?
>   (She starts to close the door, sword notwith-
>   standing.)
I want to see your girlfriend.

JULIE

She's busy.

JOE

Tell her I'm here.

JULIE

You're pathetic.
>   (Closing the door on his sword)

JOE

Hey!

(They struggle, and JULIE has almost closed the door when suddenly JO appears. JO is a large butch woman, dressed as Juliet's nurse.)

JO

What the hell is going on here? Julie, what's going on?
(She sees the three men.)
Who are these jokers?

JULIE

One of them is my ex. He's stalking me.

JOE

I am not!

JO

(To JULIE)
Why is he wearing tights?

JOE

I'm Romeo!

JO

Yeah, and I'm Juliet.

JOE

Send me your Romeo and I'll prove it!

BEN

Oh, man…

JOE

(Yelling)
Romeo! Oh, Romeo! Wherefore the hell art thou?

BEN

Hey, come on…
>(Suddenly ROZ appears in the doorway, looking adorable in her Romeo costume.)

ROZ

Julie, what is going on here—
>(She sees the three men.)
Who are they?

JO

It's Romeo and his pals. They want to see whose sword is bigger.

JULIE

Roz, this is Joe. Joe, this is Roz.

ROZ

>(Studying him)
You're not as tall as I imagined.
>(To JULIE)
Does he always wear tights?

JOE

>(To JULIE)
Does she always wear men's clothes?

ROZ

When I have a show to do.

JOE

Funny, I've got one, too.

ROZ

Really? You're still running even after our review?

JOE

Hey! The only reason they reviewed your show instead
of ours is because it's a freak show—bunch of dykes
running around with socks in their pants—

ROZ

Jealous, are we?

JOE

No, I'm not jealous. Am I?
        (He turns to BEN and MARK.)
We just thought you girls might like to do a little
sparring before the show—a kind of pre-show warm-up.
How about it, "Romeo?"

ROZ

        (To JOE)
You want to fight me?

JULIE

        (To JOE)
You are such a jerk...

JOE

        (To ROZ)
...Unless you're afraid...?

JULIE

        (To JOE)
Oh, I can't believe you—

ROZ

        (Stepping onto the stoop)
I'm not afraid.

JULIE

(To ROZ)
You're not really going to fight him, are you?

ROZ

Why not?

JULIE

Because he's an idiot.

ROZ

It'll be good practice.

JOE

That's right.
(To JULIE)
It's a "guy thing."

ROZ

Bring it!

They draw swords and
fight. Their skills are
evenly matched and
evenly amateur, as they
have both had two weeks
of stagefighting classes.
JOE wins, just barely.

JOE

(Gloating)
Want to go again?

ROZ

I'd love to, but I need to save my energy for the show.
We're expecting a full house tonight.
(Turning back to him)
It's amazing what a great review will do for your box
office.

JOE

We don't really need it. You see, our audiences know
what to expect from us.

ROZ

Apparently. I hear your houses are almost empty.

JOE

Better to have a small, but discriminating audience than
a group of ignorant thrill-seekers looking for the nearest
drag king bar.

ROZ

I think you forget Shakespeare wrote for a company that
cross-dressed all the women's roles.

JOE

That was an Elizabethan convention.

ROZ

And ours is a post-modern convention.

JOE

Gimmick.

ROZ

Convention.

                              JOE

Gimmick.

                              ROZ

Convention.
          (They draw swords and fight again, this time
          with a little more verve. ROZ trips, and JOE is
          moving in for the "kill," when JULIE intercepts
          him with a keychain can of pepper spray.)

                              JULIE

          (Bracing herself)
Back off!

                              JOE

          (Freezing in shock)
What?

                              JULIE

I said, *"Back off!"*

                              JOE

Excuse me—We're fighting.

                              JULIE

So am I. And I just won.

                              JOE

No. No, you didn't.

                              JULIE

Yes, I did.

                              JOE

That's not fighting.

JULIE

Who says?

JOE

That's not fair! You can't use pepper spray!

JULIE

Try me.

JOE

(To BEN)
She can't use pepper spray!

BEN

I wouldn't bet on it.

JOE

But that's not fair!

JULIE

Why not? It's a weapon.

JOE

(To BEN and MARK)
See? This is feminism. Right here. This is feminism in
action. This is her idea of a fair fight. The guy has to use
a sword, but the girl gets to use a can of pepper spray
that can nail him fifteen feet away. Yeah...Real equal.

JULIE

Works for me.

JOE

Come on, Ben. Tell her.

BEN

You started it, man.

JOE

You're telling me it's a fair fight when all she has to do is push a little button, and I'm choking and blind and vomiting all over the sidewalk?

BEN

That's how women fight, man. Good thing, too.

JOE

How can you say that?

BEN

They live in a different world from us, dude.

JOE

Oh, come on! It's just as dangerous for a guy. I've been mugged—twice!

JO

(Interrupting)
You want a real fight?

JOE

Yeah!

JO

Roz, give me your sword.

ROZ

No.

JO

What do you mean, "no?" Somebody's got to kick his skinny ass. You couldn't do it.

70

ROZ

I tripped. Come on, Jo. It's almost showtime.

JOE

"Joe?" Your name is Joe?

JO

Yeah. My name is Jo.

JOE

Man, you dykes have to copy everything, don't you?
Can't even come up with your own names!

JO

I'll fight you for your name.

JOE

How's that work?

JO

Whoever wins gets to rename the loser.

JOE

Deal.

ROZ

No! No more fighting!

JO
(Ignoring ROZ, she turns to BEN)
Let me have your sword.

JOE
(To BEN)
Do it!

BEN

Aw, Joe...

JOE

(Taking BEN's sword and handing it to JO)
Let's go.
>(The two begin to fence. JOE is no match for
>JO, who is obviously a skilled fighter. In no
>time, she has him on the ground, her sword
>pointed at his chest.)

JO

Say, "Juliet."
>(JOE resists.)
I said, "Say 'Juliet'!" That's your new name—
>(Suddenly MARK steps forward, drawing his
>sword.)

MARK

En garde!

JO

What's this? You want to fight? Who is this masked
man?

MARK

"Mercutio" to you!

JO

Well, bite my thumb, "Mercutio"—Let's go!
>(MARK and JO begin to fight. They are both
>highly skilled martial artists, and this is a
>prolonged fight. JO taunts him as they fight:)
Well...So the masked man can fight.

MARK

Don't patronize me.

JO

Who are you?

MARK

"A rose by any other name…"

JO

…would smell better than either one of us. Who are you?

MARK

You'll have to kill me first!
> (JO surprises MARK, disarming him and taking him down.)

JO

Unmask!
> (MARK refuses, and JO rips off his mask. After a moment of stunned silence, she begins to laugh.)

JOE

What's so funny?
> (JO ignores her and continues to laugh.)
What's so funny?

JO

Your little "Mercutio" here…He's a girl!

MARK

> (Getting up quickly)

No, I'm not!

JO

Yes, you are. I've seen you around the women's bars.

JOE

What?

MARK

(To JOE)
It's not true!

JO

Yeah? Then prove it!

MARK

(A long moment)
I'm transgender.

JO

Code for "homophobic lesbian."

MARK

No, I'm not!

JOE

Are you a man or are you a woman?

MARK

I'm a man.

JO

(Sarcastic)
"Trapped in a woman's body?"

JOE

(Disgusted)
Shit…

JOE (cont'd)
(He turns to go, but MARK pursues him.)

MARK

It's a social construct!
(To BEN)
Hey, tell him!

BEN

(Shaking his head)
I don't know, man. I don't go for that macho bullshit.

JOE

(To BEN)
It's cool, man. Don't argue with him...with her.

MARK

Him!

JO

Her!

MARK

(Grabbing his sword and menacing JO)
I'm not a lesbian!

JO

That's right! You don't have the balls—
(She rips off her skirt. She's got soccer shorts on underneath.)

ROZ

Stop it! Stop it right now! Jo, if you don't put your costume back on and come into the theatre right now, you're fired!

JO

What's the matter, Roz? Afraid that Juliet's Nurse
would make a better Romeo?

ROZ

No.

JO

I think you are.

JULIE

There's more to playing Romeo than fencing!

JO

Like what? Acting? As if you'd know anything about
that.

JULIE

What do you mean?

JO

We all know how you got the part.

JULIE

I *auditioned* for it.

JO

Is that what you call it?

ROZ

Hey—

JO

(Cutting her off)
I've got a better resume than anybody here. I think I've
got a better resume than all of you put together, so
playing Romeo must not be about the acting. And we

JO (cont'd)

know it's not about the fighting... So is it about being a
lover?
(Sizing up the two Romeos)
Well, I've definitely gone to bed with more women than
either of you... But that's not it, is it? It's really about
looks, isn't it? Can't have a big old dyke playing
Romeo, can you? Not even if I'm the strongest, and the
handsomest, and the studliest, and the best fighter. No,
you need a pretty-boy, don't you, to play Romeo?
(Looking at JOE)
Or a little femme who looks adorable in her little tights.
(Looking at ROZ)

ROZ

You said you *wanted* to play the Nurse!

JO

It's better than Lady Capulet. Those were my choices,
weren't they?
(A pause)
Your all-women theatre company...Look at you!
(Turning to JULIE)
And you! Nothing new here. Cute girls on stage. Doing
Romeo and Juliet, the biggest het show in the canon.
Yeah, so here's this radical women's theatre company
out to prove we can tell this stupid story as well as the
boys' theatres. Yeah. Great. Well, let me tell you this—
you're never gonna change the world until you change
the story. And that story's not going to change until you
recognize that women like me out-Romeo any Romeo
here. And we don't have to pretend we're men to do it!

MARK

I'm not pretending anything! I'm transgender!

JO

You just can't stand to think of yourself as female, can you? That's just about the worst thing in the world, isn't it?

MARK

Gender is a cultural construct.

JO

Don't make me laugh! Being a woman is a biological fact. Ask Julie here about her pepper spray.

MARK

You're just ignorant and transphobic.

JO

You're self-hating and lesbophobic.

> This is a fight to the death. The two draw swords and fight as if their lives depend on it. This should be the longest, most creative, and most dangerous fight of the evening. MARK is defeated and disarmed by JO. JO turns to the others for acknowledgement of her victory. ROZ and JOE, in a standard response to butch prowess, pretend to ignore it.

ROZ

Come on, Julie.

ROZ (cont'd)
(Turning to JO)
Jo, now that I know how much you hate the part, I'll
have the stage manager read it. You're fired.

JOE
(To MARK)
Yeah, Mark...or whatever your name is...You're fired,
too. I don't need drag kings to get an audience.

BEN
(Embarrassed by JOE's bigotry)
Come on, Joe...Nobody's going to know.

JOE
That's not the point! It's about artistic integrity.

BEN
So, he's transgender.

JOE
Yeah, fine. And let him find a transgender theatre
company.

JO
A plague on both your houses!
        (ROZ and JULIE exit back into the theatre, and
        BEN and JOE exit down the alley. JO returns
        MARK's sword.)
Here.

MARK
What are we supposed to do now?

JO
We're supposed to kill each other over whether it's

JO (cont'd)
better to pass as Mercutio or settle for ugly-women
character roles. That's what we're *supposed* to do...

MARK
Yeah, well, I'd rather play Mercutio than wear that
shit…
> (Indicating the padding and long skirt that JO has
> discarded)

JO
Yeah, and I'll put on a tutu before I stuff a sock down
my pants.

MARK
You don't get it.

JO
You don't get it.
> (MARK starts for his sword, but JO lays a
> restraining hand on his arm.)
"C."

MARK
See what?

JO
"C," as in "none of the above."

MARK
What's that supposed to mean?

JO
It means when people tell you to pick "A" or "B," and
you don't like either of the choices, you go for "C: None
of the above."

MARK

Yeah, but what if there is no "C."

JO

Then you have to make one.

MARK

Yeah, but you're a lesbian. That's a woman. That's an
"A" or a "B."
  (JO can't think of a response. MARK indicates
  his body.)
This feels like a costume to me, you know? I look in the
mirror, and it's always a shock. Like this can't be mine.
And what are these doing here?
  (Indicating the breasts)
They're like a prosthesis or something. I mean, it's a
mistake. That's what it feels like. I tried to walk like a
girl, and I tried to talk like a girl...I mean I *practiced*.
You think I wanted to be different when I was a kid?
You think I liked being called names ever since I can
remember? I had to fight every fucking day in fifth
grade. The boys didn't want me because I was a girl, and
the girls didn't want me because I wasn't a girl.

JO

I've got the same story.
  (A pause)
You know what I did when I was a kid?

MARK

What?

JO

I learned all the lines of Cyrano. Practiced for hours up
in my room with a curtain rod for a sword. Yeah.

JO (cont'd)
(She looks at MARK.)
I was going to be the greatest Cyrano there ever was,
because I knew what it felt like...you know, having to
fight all the time because of the way you look. Yeah...
I was going to be Cyrano...Oh, yeah...
(She laughs bitterly.)

MARK

But you never got to do it.
(JO is quiet.)
That sucks, man.

JO

I never got to do a lot of things. But that doesn't mean
I'm going to cross over to the enemy.

MARK

Men aren't my enemy.

JO

Well, you be sure and tell them that.

MARK

Just because people don't understand trans, that's no
reason for me not to live my life. I mean, the world is
homophobic, and you're still a dyke, right?

JO

Yeah, but when I fight for my identity, at least I'm
fighting with the women.

MARK

You be sure and tell them that.

JO

And I've got this body. It's the only one I'm going to
get. Cutting it up and dosing it with steroids isn't going
to change anything. It's still going to be a female body.
Except it's going to be one that's mutilated and
poisoned.

MARK

(Shaking his head)
You don't get it.

JO

All that money, all that pain, all that fucking dependence
on the medical shit...the complications... *You* don't get
it.

MARK

(Smiling)
You're jealous of me, aren't you?

JO

No...
(A pause. JO looks at MARK.)
Yeah...Yeah, I'm a little jealous. But it's not why you
think.

MARK

What do you know about what I think?

JO

I'm jealous that you think it's that easy.

MARK

Easy? What about "the money, the pain..."

83

JO

Yeah, easy. I can get money and I can deal with pain.
And I wish I believed that was all it would take. But
what kind of a man would I be?
(She looks at MARK.)
A good one?

MARK

Depends on if you want to be.

JO

Yeah? And just what would it mean for me to be a
"good man?" I know what it means to be a good dyke.
I'm a great dyke. I love women. Lesbians trust me,
because I'm one of them. I've got their back and they've
got mine. But what kind of a straight man would I
make? One that used to be a woman, and then chose not
to be? Someone raised with all that hell that women are
supposed to put up with their whole lives, and I'm going
to get indemnity because I happen to be born with a face
that could pass? How's a woman—a lesbian—whose
been afraid of men all her life going to feel about me
then?

MARK

That's her problem.

JO

See, that's where it's easy for you.

MARK

You think you're a woman, and that works for you, fine,
but don't try to lay your trip on me, man. That's not who
I am.

JO

Yeah.

    (A long silence)

MARK

What are you doing?

JO

I was thinking.

MARK

    (Defensively)
What?

JO

About Romeo and Juliet.

MARK

Shit... You know Mercutio was gay.

JO

And Juliet wore the pants. Who knows, if she'd lived long enough…

MARK

Yeah, but she's dead.

JO

So's Mercutio.

MARK

Only the good die young.

JO

What if the straight people all died in the play?

MARK

I'd like to see that.

JO

What if the women didn't have to be scared of men, and
the men didn't have to treat women like shit to feel like
they were men? Would you still want surgery?

MARK

Maybe...maybe not...but would you still want to call
yourself a woman?

JO

Why don't we tell that story and find out?

MARK

Tell it?

JO

Write our own play. Write that world where all the
straight people have to fit themselves into our model.
Where they're the ones having to get the surgeries and
having to learn how to move like a human being,
because they're not as whole as we are. Where we call
them "one-spirit" like they're freaks, because they don't
know what it's like to be born in a body that feels like
"other."

MARK

Man, I can't even imagine that play...

JO

Why not?

MARK

Just...hard to imagine.

JO

It could start with two actors who got kicked out of
Romeo and Juliet.

MARK

No way.
          (JO looks at him.)
You're serious.

JO

Why not?

MARK

Man, nobody would come to see a play about us.

JO

Yeah , but look—for two hours we could play ourselves.
For two hours we could live in a world the way we want
it to be. That's two hours more than we're ever going to
get in this lifetime.

MARK

You got that right.

JO

Truce?

MARK

Truce.

JO rises and collects her
sword. MARK is watch-
ing her. JO turns slowly
and smiles. Gleefully,
MARK grabs his sword
and the two begin to spar.

(BLACKOUT)

THE END

Entr'acte, **or**
The Night Eva Le Gallienne Was Raped

A Play in One Act

Play Summary

In October 1923, Eva Le Gallienne was raped in her
dressing room during the Broadway run of *Liliom*, a
play in which she performed the role of Julie Jordan, the
battered girlfriend of an abusive, alcoholic carousel
operator.

Entr'acte takes place in the private sanatorium on the
night of the rape, after Eva has checked herself in. In a
state of post-traumatic hyper-arousal, she waits for a
"friend" to arrive.

The friend is Mimsey Benson, Eva's former lover
and fellow-actor, who left her ten months earlier for the
security of a heterosexual marriage. Eva has not seen
Mimsey since the breakup.

In this charged environment, the two women
confront their feelings for each other, and Mimsey, who
had lost her identity in her former relationship with Eva,
walks a tightrope between compassion for the young
women and the detachment necessary to protect herself
from Eva's overwhelming neediness.

This play is a tour-de-force for a young actor (Eva is
twenty-three). In the space of the thirty-minute drama,
Eva runs a gamut of extreme dissociative states as she
moves through denial, bargaining, rage, and grief to
finally arrive at acceptance of her losses. Making rapid
transitions, she is alternately the abandoned lover, the
imperious Broadway star, the enraged child, the dazzling
performer, the terrified victim, the skillful seductress,
and the visionary entrepreneur who will go on to found
the legendary Civic Repertory Theatre.

The interpersonal drama of the two women is
punctuated by interactions with two of the nurses on the
staff, one of them an adoring fan of Eva's and the other a
hard-nosed pragmatist. Balancing between the two poles
represented by the nurses, Eva and Mimsey struggle to

91

create a new relationship toward each other and toward
their art.

Four women
Thirty minutes
Single set

Cast of Characters

Head Nurse: A woman in her fifties.

Aide: A young woman in her late teens.

Eva Le Gallienne: A young woman of twenty-three.

Mimsey Benson: A woman in her mid-thirties.

Scene
A private room in Mackie's Sanatorium, New York City.

Time
Very late one night in October, 1923.

Entr'acte

Setting: A private room in
Mackie's Sanatorium in
New York City. There is a
single bed in the room,
and next to it, a small
table with a pitcher of
water and a glass. Also
next to the bed is a chair
with clothing folded on it.
The curtains of the
window are pulled shut,
and the room is dimly lit.
It is an October night,
1923.

At Rise: There is a patient in the
bed, but her face is hidden
from the audience. The
door opens, and the
HEAD NURSE enters,
carrying a clipboard and a
bottle of pills. The HEAD
NURSE is extremely
competent at her job and
does not suffer fools
gladly.

               The HEAD NURSE
checks on the patient, who
is sleeping. She looks at
her watch and marks
something on her
clipboard. Crossing to the
table by the bed, she

counts out two pills and
sets them on the tray. Her
back is to the door.

The AIDE peers through
the door and then enters
furtively. She is a very
young woman, passionate
in her commitment to
romantic ideals. She has
done what she can with
her hair and her makeup to
compensate for the
drabness of her uniform.

The AIDE crosses quietly
to the bed. Turning, the
HEAD NURSE sees her.

HEAD NURSE

(Whispering)
What are you doing here?

AIDE

I wanted to look at her.

HEAD NURSE

She's not your patient.

AIDE

But it's Eva Le Gallienne!

HEAD NURSE
(Placing herself between the AIDE and the
patient.)
It doesn't matter who it is. She's not your patient.

AIDE

But I just want to look at her!

HEAD NURSE

You can look at your own patients.

AIDE

But none of them are famous actresses like Miss Le Gallienne. I just want to see her face.

HEAD NURSE

No!
   (The AIDE suddenly notices the clothing on the chair. She crosses to it ecstatically.)

AIDE

Oh, look!

HEAD NURSE

What?
   (The AIDE is holding up various pieces of clothing.)
What are you doing?

AIDE

It's her costume—the one I saw her wear in her show! She plays this peasant girl. Oh, look—here's her head scarf! And the shoes!
   (She picks up a pair of battered black boots.)
These are her shoes! Oh!

HEAD NURSE

Put those down!

AIDE

She must have come right from the theatre. She didn't
even take the time to change.

HEAD NURSE

Put those down!
> (The AIDE sets the boots tenderly on the floor.)

AIDE

She must have come right from the theatre. She didn't
even take the time to change.

HEAD NURSE

Put those down!
> (The AIDE sets the boots tenderly on the floor.)

AIDE

What's Eva Le Gallienne doing in a private sanatorium?

HEAD NURSE

None of your business.

AIDE

Did you see them bring her in?

HEAD NURSE

She brought herself in a taxi sometime after midnight.
Now, go back to your floor.

AIDE

And you don't know why she's here?

HEAD NURSE

I know why she's here, but I'm not going to tell *you*.

AIDE

Well, I think I know. When a famous actress checks
herself into a sanatorium in the middle of the night, it
can only be one thing.
(The HEAD NURSE looks at her.)
The angst.

HEAD NURSE

The what?

AIDE

(Matter-of-factly)
Angst... You know—the passion, the torment—all that
unrequited love. After a while, it just gets to be more
than they can handle, so they either go crazy or they kill
themselves.

HEAD NURSE

You've got it all figured out.

AIDE

Well, I've seen Miss Le Gallienne act. In fact, I've seen
her show three times since it opened this spring, and
anyone playing Julie the way Miss Le Gallienne plays
her is bound to break down. I mean, the way Julie loves
her boyfriend—his name is Liliom—that's the name of
the play, too.. Anyway, he's this man who runs the
carousel in the park, and he's really mean to her. He
never says he loves her. But Julie never says she loves
him, either, except that you just know that she does,
because of the way she looks at him and the way she
never says anything bad about him, even when he's
drinking and acting mean. And then, even after he's
dead, she just goes right on loving him. It's so beautiful.
(She has picked up the boots again.)

HEAD NURSE

Put those down!

AIDE

And then every night at the very end of the show, Julie turns to her daughter—it's his daughter, too, only he died before Julie could tell him she was pregnant—but, anyway, at the very end of the show, Julie turns to her daughter and she says...
    (Imitating EVA's delivery)
"It is possible, dear—that someone may beat you and beat you and beat you, and not hurt you at all."
    (The HEAD NURSE turns away, but the AIDE
    grabs her arm.)
No, but she means it!

HEAD NURSE

I've nursed a lot of beaten women, and they hurt plenty.

AIDE

But Julie loves Liliom so much, she doesn't feel it when he hits her.

HEAD NURSE

That's make-believe.

AIDE

No, it isn't! If you love someone enough, they can't hurt you.

HEAD NURSE

This Julie loved too much for her own good, if you ask me.
    (EVA moans and starts to turn over.)

100

AIDE

It's her!
(She starts to cross to the bed, but the HEAD
NURSE blocks her.)

HEAD NURSE

Leave her alone! She's not your patient!

AIDE

I just want to look at her!

HEAD NURSE

(Driving her out)
You can look at her when she's play-acting. Now, go on!
Get back to your floor before I write you up.

> The HEAD NURSE
> pushes the AIDE out of
> the room and closes the
> door. EVA sits up,
> temporarily confused.
>
> EVA is twenty-three. She
> wears a hospital gown,
> and her hair is unruly. She
> is in a post-traumatic state
> of hyper-arousal.

EVA

Who are you?

HEAD NURSE

I'm the nurse on duty for the night shift.

EVA

Did the doctor talk to you?

HEAD NURSE
(Crossing to the table)
He left before I came on.

EVA
(Relieved)
I'm just here for a few days of rest. That's all I'm here
for. And I don't want anyone to know I'm here,
especially the newspapers. Do you understand?

HEAD NURSE
(Not one to be taking orders from her patients,
    the HEAD NURSE holds out the pills.)
You need to take these.

EVA
What are they?

HEAD NURSE
Sedatives. The doctor said to give them to you if you
woke up before morning.

EVA
What time is it?

HEAD NURSE
Three-twenty. Take them.

EVA
No! I can't. I'm expecting someone.

HEAD NURSE
Doctor's orders, no visitors.

EVA

But I've asked someone to come.

HEAD NURSE

(Checking the chart)
"No visitors."

EVA

Let me speak with the doctor.

HEAD NURSE

He won't be here until morning.

EVA

You'll have to call him.

HEAD NURSE

Take the pills.

EVA

I need to speak with your supervisor.

HEAD NURSE

I'm the nurse in charge of the night shift.

EVA

(Trying a different approach)
Please—this is very, very important. I've left a message
for a friend...
(The HEAD NURSE is unimpressed.)
She's my *best* friend. We lived together for three years .
I've asked her to bring me something.

HEAD NURSE

Then she can leave it at the front desk.

EVA

But I *have* to see her. It's very important. I haven't seen
her in almost a year!
(Suddenly there is a knock. EVA starts.)
Mimsey!

HEAD NURSE

(Calling out)
What is it?
(The AIDE opens the door and begins to enter,
but the HEAD NURSE crosses quickly to her,
preventing her from entering and blocking her
view of EVA.)

AIDE

(Trying to see around the HEAD NURSE)
There's a visitor here for Miss Le—for the patient in
room 326.

EVA

(Excited)
It's Mimsey!

HEAD NURSE

(To the AIDE)
Who is it?

AIDE

(She turns to speak with someone offstage before
responding.)
A "Mrs. Stuart Benson."
(EVA has a strong reaction to this response.)

HEAD NURSE

(To EVA)
Is this your friend?

EVA

(Struggling)

Yes.

HEAD NURSE

(To EVA)

I'm going to let her come in, but she can only stay a minute. Doctor's orders.

> EVA is focused on the door. The HEAD NURSE opens the door wide, revealing MIMSEY, a woman in her mid-thirties, tastefully and expensively dressed. She carries a large bag. MIMSEY is temporarily framed in the glare of the hallway.

HEAD NURSE

(To MIMSEY)

She's not supposed to have any visitors. I'm going to let you see her, but you can't stay.

> The HEAD NURSE starts to exit, pushing the AIDE back. Just before she closes the door, she switches on the light in the room. The two women look at each other in silence for a moment. EVA speaks first.

EVA

(Challenging MIMSEY)
"Mrs. Stuart Benson?"

MIMSEY

(Caught up in her own concerns, MIMSEY does
not hear EVA's taunt.)
Are you all right?

EVA

Did you bring Bessie?

MIMSEY

Yes. She's in the bag.
(EVA holds out her arms for the bag, and
MIMSEY hands it to her.)
Eva, what happened? Are you all right? The doorman
gave me your message as soon as I got in...

> EVA has taken out the
> doll. Bessie is a fancy
> European doll from the
> turn-of-the-century. Her
> head, however, is made
> from a sock on which a
> face and hair have been
> crudely drawn in black
> ink. EVA closes her eyes
> and embraces the doll.

MIMSEY

What happened? Were you in an accident?
(EVA ignores her.)
Eva!

EVA

(Opening her eyes)
Nothing.
(MIMSEY doesn't understand.)
Nothing happened. I just needed to get away from the
show for a few days. I needed to go somewhere the
reporters wouldn't find me.
(She smiles cheerfully at MIMSEY.)
I'm fine. Really.
(MIMSEY says nothing. EVA becomes
conversational.)
How are you?

MIMSEY

It's three in the morning! I thought something terrible
had happened. I've been running all over the city, going
to your apartment to get Bessie—I didn't know what had
happened. I thought you might be dying!

EVA

(Defensively)
You know how much Bessie means to me. I needed her.

MIMSEY

(Becoming angry)
Did it occur to you that your message would scare me to
death? Why didn't you just telephone me in the
morning?

EVA

Because this way, I knew you'd come.

MIMSEY

You did this on purpose?
(MIMSEY turns to leave.)

EVA

Well, it's true, isn't it? You wouldn't have come if you
didn't think it was an emergency.

MIMSEY

(Turning)
What ever gave you that idea?

EVA

You didn't come to my opening.

MIMSEY

I didn't come to your opening, because I didn't think
you'd want me to be there.

EVA

Why?

MIMSEY

Because—
(She stops herself.)

EVA

Because of Stuart? Because of your husband? You
thought my opening night on Broadway, I would be
thinking about whether or not you brought your *husband*
with you?

MIMSEY

(Stiffening)
I didn't know what you'd do.

EVA

I wouldn't have even *noticed*. Believe it or not, I was
busy acting. Julie—remember? The role I wanted to get
two years ago—the one we used to rehearse together

EVA (cont'd)
with you being Marie—remember? You played my best
friend, and we talked about being in the show together.
(MIMSEY says nothing.)
I could have gotten you into the show. I could have.

MIMSEY
That's not the point.

EVA
I could still do it.
(MIMSEY shakes her head in disbelief.)
Did you read my notices?
(MIMSEY turns to leave.)
Mimsey?

MIMSEY
What?

EVA
(Urgent)
It *was* an emergency.
(MIMSEY waits.)
It's about Bessie.
(MIMSEY turns again to leave.)
Please—please, listen, Mimsey. It *is* an emergency.
Please—
(During this speech, MIMSEY keeps trying to
interrupt.)
Remember how I told you about my Nanny, and how
she gave me Bessie on my third birthday, after my
parents separated? And how, before I ever even looked
at it, I threw it out of my carriage, and the head smashed
on the pavement? And remember how I told you Nanny
made a new head out of a sock, and she painted a face
on it with India ink—and how, after that, every time

109

EVA (cont'd)
Bessie needed a new head, Nanny would take a new
sock—

MIMSEY
(Shouting)
Eva, it's almost four—

EVA
(Escalating)
But it's like that, Mimsey! It's like that! I just keep
getting new heads over and over again, like Bessie. No
one knows what I really look like! No one has ever seen
my real face! *I* don't even know what I look like!
(MIMSEY begins to laugh, shaking her head.)
What? What's funny?

MIMSEY
I had forgotten what it was like living with you.

EVA
(Mistaking the laughter for a positive sign)
Do you miss me?

MIMSEY
(Serious again)
Eva, I have to go.

EVA
(With bitterness)
Back to your "husband?"

MIMSEY
(Evenly)
Yes.

EVA
Do you sleep together in the same bed, like we did?

MIMSEY

Good-bye, Eva.

EVA

You're leaving me again.

MIMSEY

(Smiling)
You've got Bessie.

EVA

(Appealingly)
Will you come back and see me?

MIMSEY

(Wary)
I don't know.

EVA

I'm all alone.

MIMSEY

What about your mother?

EVA

She went back to Europe when the show opened. It's
your fault, she's gone. If it hadn't been for you, I would
have been living with her.

MIMSEY

Eva, you moved out from her three years ago.

EVA

So I could live with you! Now you're the only family I
have.

MIMSEY

Your father is here in New York.

EVA

You know I never see him.

MIMSEY

You could if you wanted to.

EVA

My father? Do you know why I never see him?

MIMSEY

Because your mother didn't want you to.

EVA

Do you know why?

MIMSEY

(Exasperated)
I don't know why. I suppose there was another woman—

EVA

Another woman?
    (EVA starts laughing.)

MIMSEY

You told me she had walked in on some kind of situation...

EVA

The situation she walked in on was my father and me! I was three years old. Mimsey, I was the "other woman."

MIMSEY

(Shocked)
I'm sorry, Eva. I didn't know.

EVA

(Matter-of-factly)
Well, now you do.

MIMSEY

I'm sorry.

EVA

(Shrugging it off)
I don't remember anything about it.
(Looking at Bessie)
I must have gotten a different head.
(MIMSEY doesn't say anything.)
You're my family now.
(A pause)
You're the only friend I have.

MIMSEY

(Smiling)
I don't believe that.

EVA

(Defensive)
You mean Alla?

MIMSEY

I don't mean anyone in particular. I just know that you
have a lot of friends. You always have.

EVA

(Desperate to engage her)
You think Alla Nazimova and I were lovers, don't you?
You've always thought that. You were always

113

EVA (cont'd)

jealous of her, but you're wrong about us. And the only reason I went to see her after you left was to get away from New York. It was your fault.

(MIMSEY shakes her head.)

She wasn't interested in me at all. She had another girlfriend! You can ask her. She never even looked at me.

(MIMSEY laughs.)

It's true! Ask her! I was always faithful!

MIMSEY

No, I believe you. You *have* always been faithful, Eva. Your one love is the theatre, and everyone else is a mistress.

EVA

That's not true. I loved you! We lived together for three years. Didn't I arrange it so you could go on tours with me?

(MIMSEY shakes her head.)

I did!

MIMSEY

Eva, I was an *understudy* and you were the star.

EVA

So? We were together.

MIMSEY

Would you have understudied for me, if I had been the star?

EVA

Yes!

MIMSEY

(Shaking her head)
Oh, Eva, you really *don't* know who you are, do you?

EVA

But *you* know who I am. That's why I need you,
Mimsey.

MIMSEY

(Quietly)
Eva, it's over.

EVA

(Angry)
Over for you, but it'll never be over for me. You had no
right to leave the way you did...sneaking around behind
my back while I was on tour—waiting until I got back to
tell me—
(MIMSEY crosses toward the door. EVA
escalates.)
...like a *coward*! And it's your fault I'm here! It's your
fault! If we were still together, you would have been at
the theatre tonight! You would have been waiting for me
in my dressing room!
(She jumps out of bed, pursuing MIMSEY.)
*You would have been in my dressing room and it
wouldn't have happened!*

MIMSEY

(Turning)
What wouldn't have happened?

EVA

(Stopping suddenly)
You would have been in my dressing room.

MIMSEY

What happened in your dressing room tonight?

EVA

(Suddenly frightened, she begins to cry.)

It's your fault. It's all your fault. It's all your fault.

(MIMSEY watches her in shock. EVA crosses
to the clothing on the chair.)

But it wasn't me. It was Julie. It was *her*. It was *Julie*.

(To MIMSEY, pleadingly)

I was still wearing Julie's clothes.

(Turning back to the chair.)

It was Julie. He did it to Julie.

(She picks up the clothes, and then screams and
throws them down as if they have suddenly
become alive. She turns and pushes her face into
the bed.)

It was Julie...It was Julie...It was Julie.

MIMSEY

(Alarmed)

Eva, what happened tonight?

EVA

(Face still in the mattress)

It was Julie...It was Julie...It was Julie.

MIMSEY

(Asking quietly)

What happened to Julie?

(She crosses behind EVA.)

Eva, tell me what happened.

EVA

(Turning violently on her)

You don't care!

116

EVA (cont'd)

(Mocking her)

It's the middle of the night! Your husband's waiting for you! You don't care!

MIMSEY

I *do* care.

EVA

(Pausing to look at her, as if for the first time)

You *like* it, don't you? You let Stuart do that every night—and twice on Sunday, don't you? Don't you? You let Stuart do it, don't you? Get away from me! Get away from me!

    (MIMSEY moves to restrain her, but EVA beats
    her away with the doll. The doll's head flies off.
    EVA is screaming.)

Don't touch me! Don't you ever touch me again!

    (MIMSEY backs off. EVA becomes calmer.)

It's your fault. It's all your fault.

    (Just then, there is a knock.)

AIDE

(Offstage)

Miss Le Gallienne?

    (MIMSEY leaves EVA and crosses quickly to
    the door, intending to protect EVA. She opens it
    a crack. The AIDE speaks very rapidly.)

I don't mean to bother you, but I've seen Miss Le Gallienne's show three times, and I was wondering if I could just meet her—

MIMSEY

No, I'm sorry—

    (She starts to close the door, but EVA
    interrupts.)

EVA

Wait! Let her in.
    (MIMSEY looks at EVA, who has suddenly
    become very cool and in control.)
Let her in.

                        MIMSEY opens the door
                        in a gesture of resignation.
                        The AIDE enters. EVA, in
                        all her disheveled glory,
                        sits enthroned on the bed
                        amidst the tangle of
                        snarled bedding. The
                        AIDE stares at her idol in
                        awe.

EVA

You wanted to see me?
    (The AIDE is speechless. EVA turns to
    MIMSEY, who is still standing by the door.)
She's seen my play three times.
    (Turning to the AIDE)
This is my best friend. She's never seen it even once.

AIDE

    (Turning to MIMSEY)
Oh, you should go! It's wonderful! It's the most beautiful
thing in the world the way Julie—that's Miss Le
Gallienne—loves Liliom.

EVA

    (To MIMSEY)
Did you hear that? She loves the way I love Liliom.
Even though he leaves me right when I need him the
most.

AIDE

Oh, yes. That's when you know she *really* loves him. He
could do anything—

EVA

(Interrupting)
Yes, he could. And Julie will just keep loving him, won't
she?

AIDE

Oh, yes. You know she will.

EVA

(Pleasantly)
And you don't think that's stupid of her?

AIDE

(Rapturously)
Oh, no! It's the most beautiful thing in the world.

> EVA begins to laugh
> hysterically, throwing the
> pillows around. The
> AIDE, startled, looks first
> at EVA and then at
> MIMSEY. She laughs
> uncertainly. The HEAD
> NURSE bursts into the
> room.

HEAD NURSE

(To the AIDE)
What are you doing in here?

AIDE

Miss Le Gallienne invited me in.

HEAD NURSE

I'm going to see that you're fired.

AIDE

But she asked me in.
    (To MIMSEY)
Didn't she?
    (EVA is still laughing hysterically. The AIDE
    indicates her.)
She's acting—aren't you, Miss Le Gallienne?
    (EVA does not acknowledge her, and the HEAD
    NURSE pushes the AIDE out the door. She
    turns to MIMSEY.)

HEAD NURSE

You're going to have to leave. The doctor's orders are
"no visitors."

MIMSEY

In a minute.

HEAD NURSE

No, *now*.
    (EVA has stopped laughing. She watches
    MIMSEY attentively.)

MIMSEY

I'm not going to leave her in this condition.

HEAD NURSE

It's you and that aide got her all upset.

120

MIMSEY

What has got her all upset is people who don't
understand her, people who don't know anything about
art or about artists. What she needs is a little love and a
little tenderness, and I'm the only one in this hospital
right now who can give her that, and I'm not leaving.
    (The HEAD NURSE turns sharply and exits,
    closing the door.)

EVA

(Now that MIMSEY has said she will stay, EVA
becomes very childlike.)
It's a farce, isn't it? We're in a farce, aren't we?
    (MIMSEY turns toward her, and then she sighs
    and crosses to the table.)

MIMSEY

What are these?

EVA

Sedatives.

MIMSEY

I want you to take them. They'll calm you down.
    (She holds them out to EVA with a glass of
    water. Obediently, EVA takes them.)
Don't say anything.
    (EVA swallows the pills.)
Drink the whole glass.
    (MIMSEY watches EVA as she drinks.)
Now just breathe slowly. I want you to breathe slowly
and don't try to talk.

> EVA does what she's told,
> and MIMSEY begins to
> pick up the clothing,
> folding it and putting it

over the back of the chair.
She tucks the sheets and
blankets back in and
collects the pillows. EVA
watches her, breathing
slowly. MIMSEY picks up
the headless Bessie and
sets her on the bed.

EVA

She lost her head again, didn't she?
(MIMSEY doesn't respond.)
Like me.
(A pause. EVA is very calm now.)
Don't you want to know who it was?

MIMSEY

Do you want to tell me?

EVA

It was an actor. I knew him.

MIMSEY

Someone in the show?
(EVA tries to answer, but the question is too
difficult. Tactfully, MIMSEY turns her attention
away by tucking the sheets into a bed corner.)

EVA

(Whispering)
Don't tell anyone.

MIMSEY

I won't.

EVA

(Thoughtfully)
It would be the end.

MIMSEY

Where else are you hurt?

EVA

(EVA is quiet and detached.)
My head. He knocked my head against the wall. And the
floor. I have some bruises.
(MIMSEY looks at her with concern.)
Will you get in the bed and hold me?
(MIMSEY hesitates)
Please...?

> MIMSEY takes off her
> shoes and gets into the bed
> behind EVA. She wraps
> her arms around her, like a
> mother with a child. EVA
> allows herself to be held
> like this for a moment, but
> then she begins nuzzling
> her face against
> MIMSEY's neck, angling
> for a kiss. MIMSEY turns
> her head away. EVA
> begins to stroke
> MIMSEY's hair, her neck,
> and then her breast.

MIMSEY

Eva, don't.
(EVA kisses her breast and MIMSEY pulls away
abruptly.)

EVA

(Quietly)
Do you really like it when he does that to you?
    (MIMSEY gets out of the bed and puts her shoes
    on.)
Do you?

MIMSEY

It's not about that. You know it's not about that.

EVA

(Petulant)
What is it about?

MIMSEY

It's about having a home.

EVA

We had a home.

MIMSEY

(Still putting on her shoes)
You were never there.

EVA

You were gone, too.

MIMSEY

Eva, you were the star. You were the one with the tours.
You were the one at all the parties.

EVA

That wasn't my fault!

MIMSEY

I didn't say it was. I just said I wanted a home. I wanted

MIMSEY (cont'd)

someone to come home to.
(EVA looks at her)
I'm thirty-four, Eva. I'm not young anymore.

EVA

Yes, you are.

MIMSEY

No, I'm not.

EVA

You could still play twenty.

MIMSEY

I don't *want* to play twenty. I don't want *play* anything. I
want to be thirty-four, and I want to have my own
home—

EVA

It's Stuart's.

MIMSEY

(With surprising vehemence)
It's *mine*.

EVA

(Taken aback, EVA pauses for a moment before
responding.)
And now *I* don't have one.

MIMSEY

The theatre's your home. It's always going to be.

EVA

Not after tonight.

EVA (cont'd)
(MIMSEY looks at her)
I can't go back. You don't think I could touch *those*
again, do you?
(She indicates the clothing on the chair.)
No.
(Shaking her head)
No, no, no, no, no, no, no.

MIMSEY

You can take some time off.

EVA

No. I'm leaving. I'm leaving the theatre.

MIMSEY

(Smiling)
But what about your famous dream? How many times
did you tell me that before you were forty you were
going to play Hamlet and Hedda—and what else? Oh,
Peter Pan...and Juliet—

EVA

And even if I went back, I could never play any of those.
I'll be playing Julie's until I'm as old as you are, and then
it'll be too late. Where could I get any training, playing
ingenues six days a week for years at a time? Nobody's
doing repertory in New York, real repertory—five
different shows a week. That's what Duse had. That's
what Bernhardt had. I'm going to end up just like you,
except *I'm* not going to prostitute myself.

MIMSEY

Eva, I need to go. I can come back if you want me to.

126

EVA

Would you?

MIMSEY

Yes, of course.

EVA

Would you come stay with me, if I went back to my apartment?

MIMSEY

For a few days.

EVA

But then you'd leave?

MIMSEY

Yes.

EVA

Then don't come back.

MIMSEY

All right, Eva.
    (She picks up her bag and turns.)
I love you.

EVA

What's the point?

MIMSEY leaves. EVA
flips the bed covers,
listlessly. She is feeling
the effects of the pills. She
picks up Bessie, crosses to
the window with the

headless doll, and pulls
open the curtains. The sky
is just starting to grow
light. EVA begins to recite
a scene from *Romeo and
Juliet*. The door is slightly
ajar.

EVA

(Mocking Juliet's denial)
Wilt thou be gone? it is not yet near day.
It was the nightingale, and not the lark,
That pierc'd the fearful hollow of thine ear;
(Beginning to warm to her part)
Nightly she sings on yond pomegranate tree.
Believe me, love, it was the nightingale…
…Yond light is not day-light, I know it, I;
It is some meteor that the sun exhal'd
To be to thee this night a torch-bearer
And light thee on thy way to Mantua.
Therefore stay yet, thou need'st not to be gone…
(EVA pauses, looking at the inevitable dawn.
She speaks the last line in her own voice.)
It is, it is! Hi hence, be gone, away!

She begins to cry. After a
moment, she is interrupted
by the sound of clapping.
The AIDE steps from
behind the door, where
she has been watching and
listening.

AIDE

(In quiet awe)
Juliet!

EVA

What are you doing here?

AIDE

I just came to say good-bye.
    (EVA doesn't say anything.)
They fired me, but I don't care. It was worth it.

EVA

Julie is a lie.

AIDE

No, she's not.

EVA

When men beat you, it hurts.

AIDE

    (Shaking her head)
No.

EVA

When people leave, it hurts.

AIDE

Not if you really love them.

EVA

And when you wake up tomorrow without a job, you're
going to be sorry.

AIDE

Never. This is the greatest day of my life. I saw Eva Le
Gallienne play *Romeo and Juliet...*and it was *beautiful!*

EVA

(EVA looks at her for a long moment, and then
turns wearily toward the window.)
Please go away.
    (The AIDE exits and MIMSEY enters.)

MIMSEY

I came back to say I'm sorry. If you need me to stay—

EVA

(Without turning)
I need a theatre.

MIMSEY

(Looking at her)
I know.

EVA

My own theatre. Like Duse. Like Bernhardt.

MIMSEY

I know, Eva.

EVA

(Facing her)
One that does repertory.
    (MIMSEY smiles. The two women look at each
other—really look at each other—for a long
moment.)
Do you think I could do it?

MIMSEY

(Serious)
If anyone in New York could do it, it would be you.

EVA

(Considering)
Do you really think so?

MIMSEY

Yes, I do.

EVA

I could start with one production—to see what kind of
support there was. What do you think?

MIMSEY

I think we can talk about it tomorrow. Why don't you go
to bed?

EVA

(She hesitates and then climbs into bed.)
I could start with *Hedda.* What do you think? Or maybe
The Master Builder. It's not as well-known, but that
might be an advantage for a first production.

MIMSEY

(Tucking her in)
I would go with *Hedda,* but, of course, you would be
compared to Duse.

EVA

I'm not afraid.

MIMSEY

No, of course not.

EVA

Mimsey, would you work with me?

MIMSEY

    (Smiling)
We'll see.
    (Kissing her on the brow)
Good-night, Eva.

EVA

You'll come tomorrow?

MIMSEY

Yes.
    (EVA turns over on her side and closes her
    eyes.)

EVA

I would need to commission a new translation.
    (She opens her eyes.)
You know the Archer is un-actable—

MIMSEY

    (Smiling to herself)
Shhh. Yes, it is.

                  MIMSEY strokes EVA's
                  head, and EVA smiles.
                  She closes her eyes, and
                  this time she does not
                  open them again.

                  After a moment,
                  MIMSEY sighs and
                  crosses to the window
                  where the headless Bessie
                  has been propped on the
                  sill. She picks her up.
                  Looking around on the

floor for the head, she
finds it and picks it up.
She places the doll next to
the sleeping EVA, setting
the head gently back in
place.

Turning out the light,
MIMSEY exits quietly as
the first rays of dawn steal
over the horizon, sending
a shaft of sunlight into the
darkened room.

(BLACKOUT)

THE END

The Pele Chant

A Civilized Conversation in One-Act

This play is dedicated to Haunani-Kay Trask,
a leader in the Native Hawai'ian sovereignty struggle.

*For so long, more than half my life, I had
misunderstood this written record, thinking it
described my own people. But my history was
nowhere present. For we had not written. We
had chanted and sailed and fished and built and
prayed. And we had told stories through the
great blood lines of memory: genealogy.*

*To know my history, I had to put away my books
and return to the land. I had to plant taro in the
earth before I could understand the inseparable
bond between people and āina. I had to feel
again the spirits of natue and take gifts of plants
and fish to the ancient altars. I had to begin to
speak of my language with our elders and leave
long silences for wisdom to grow. But before
anything else, I needed to learn the language like
a lover so that I could rock within her and lie at
night in her dreaming arms.*

–Haunani-Kay Trask

Play Summary

The play opens in 1969, with Dr. Evelyn Bateman, a white college professor, interviewing Miss Lydia Aholo, a ninety-two-year-old Native Hawaiian. Miss Aholo is the *hanai* ("adoptive") daughter of Queen Liliuokalani, the last queen of Hawai'i. Dr. Bateman is preparing to write the first Western biography sympathetic to the Queen, detailing her overthrow by the U.S. government.

During the course of the interview, Miss Aholo reveals that the Queen entrusted her with a mission before her death. She asked her adoptive daughter to answer the question that tormented her at the end of her life: "What did I do that was so wrong that I should lose my country for my dear people?"

Dr. Bateman is shocked by the question, insisting that the Queen was a helpless victim of a colonial effort that had its beginnings before she was even born. Dr. Bateman is adamant that the Queen could have done nothing to change the course of history. Miss Aholo is equally insistent that there is an answer to the Queen's question and that the future for Native people depends on an understanding of this answer.

As the Western liberal historian and the Native woman struggle with the metaphysics of language, colonization, and victimization, their collaboration begins to unravel. When Dr. Bateman recounts an anecdote about a visit to the Queen by three Native *kahunas,* or priestesses, urging her to join them in an act of civil disobedience involving the recitation of the Pele Chant, Lydia finds the answer to the Queen's question— and with it, the secret of spiritual decolonization.

Two women
Single set
Thirty minutes

Cast of Characters

<u>Lydia Aholo (Kaohohiponiponiokalani)</u>: A Native
    Hawai'ian woman, 92.

<u>Dr. Bateman</u>: A white woman, 50's.

Scene
The living room of Lydia Aholo's home in Honolulu.

Time
July 1969.

The Pele Chant

Setting: The living room of the
                        home of LYDIA AHOLO
                        in Honolulu, Hawai'i,
                        1969. The room contains a
                        mixture of Western and
                        Native furniture and
                        artifacts. There are several
                        tropical plants that have
                        been lovingly tended, and
                        maybe a vase of beautiful
                        tropical flowers. A portrait
                        of Queen Liliuokalani
                        hangs on the wall. There is
                        a photograph of the
                        caldera of Kilauea on a
                        table by Miss Aholo.

At Rise: LYDIA AHOLO, 92, sits
                        in a wheelchair. She is a
                        Native Hawai'ian, and she
                        wears a Hawai'ian floral
                        dress. She is being
                        interviewed by
                        DR.BATEMAN, 52, a
                        white college professor
                        from California. DR.
                        BATEMAN sits facing
                        LYDIA AHOLO, a
                        notebook on her lap.
                        There is a tape recorder
                        with a microphone on a
                        low table between them,
                        and on the floor by the
                        table is a box filled with

> cassette tapes that have
> already been recorded.

DR. BATEMAN
Were you with the Queen when she died?

LYDIA AHOLO
(Unaccustomed to being recorded, she speaks to
DR. BATEMAN instead of into the microphone.)
No. I had already left Hawai'i.

DR. BATEMAN
(Moving the tape recorder closer to LYDIA)
I'm sorry. Can you speak up?

LYDIA AHOLO
(Speaking up)
No. I was not with her. I had already left.

DR. BATEMAN
You left Hawai'i before she died?

LYDIA AHOLO
The Queen had sent me to the mainland, to attend
Oberlin College in Ohio.

DR. BATEMAN
(Noticing the tape)
Oh, wait...

LYDIA AHOLO
She had sent me there to study history.

DR. BATEMAN
(Fishing in the box for a new tape)
Excuse me...

LYDIA AHOLO
She wanted me to write her biography—to tell the truth
about her life—

DR. BATEMAN
Miss Aholo! Excuse me...
(LYDIA AHOLO stops.)
I'm sorry to interrupt you, but that's the end of the tape.
Just a minute...
(She changes the tape.)
I'm sorry...We're almost through.
(Turning to LYDIA)
How are you feeling? Are you tired?

LYDIA AHOLO
No. She wanted me—

DR. BATEMAN
Wait!
(She speaks into the microphone.)
This is tape number...
(Checking the label of the previous tape)
...thirty...July 13, 1969, Honolulu. This is Dr. Evelyn
Bateman, associate professor of history at California
State University, and I am interviewing Miss Lydia
Aholo, the adopted daughter of Queen Liliuokalani, the
last Queen of Hawai'i.
(Turning back to LYDIA AHOLO. LYDIA is
silent.)
Where were we?

LYDIA AHOLO

(A pause)
You were asking about the Queen's death.

DR.BATEMAN

That's right.
(Checking her notes)
And you were telling me that you were not with her when
she died.

LYDIA AHOLO

Dr. Bateman, now I must interrupt you.

DR. BATEMAN

Yes?

LYDIA AHOLO

Why do you think I agreed to this interview?

DR. BATEMAN

(Surprised)
What do you mean?

LYDIA AHOLO

You have been asking me questions about the Queen for
many months now, and I have allowed you to tape
record my answers. And yet you have never asked me
why I agreed to do that. And now I ask you if you know.

DR. BATEMAN

I thought it was obvious.
(DR. BATEMAN turns off the tape.)
I am writing the first biography of your mother that
will—

LYDIA AHOLO

(Correcting her)
My *hanai*.

DR. BATEMAN

Adoptive mother.

LYDIA

No! *Hanai* does not mean "adoptive." *Hanai* was our
custom of *sharing* children, not owning them. My father
allowed the Queen to raise me as her own daughter,
because my mother died when I was born and the Queen
could not have children. It was a *gift*—it was *aloha*.
    (A long pause)

DR. BATEMAN

You asked me why I thought you agreed to the
interview. Do you want me to answer?
    (Another long pause)
Because this will be the first Western biography of
you—of the Queen to tell the truth about how she was
betrayed—

LYDIA

But I have had fifty years, since the Queen's death, to
tell that story, and I chose not to. Why would I tell it
now?

DR. BATEMAN

Because fifty years ago it was 1919, and the world was
not ready to hear it. Twenty-five years ago it was 1944,
and we were in the middle of a war with Japan after the
bombing of Pearl Harbor, and nobody would have
listened. Ten years ago, it was 1959 and Hawaii had just
become a state, and nobody would have listened. But
today it's 1969. Today, we are fighting an unpopular

DR. BATEMAN (cont'd)
war that we are losing in Vietnam, a war that people can
watch from their living rooms for the first time, and
today people are ready to talk about U.S. imperialism.
Today there is a Civil Rights movement and an
American Indian movement, and people are having to
face the history of racism and genocide in this country.
Today, there is a movement for Women's Liberation and
people are starting to challenge the way women have
been represented in history. This is the first time since
your *hanai* mother died that people are ready to hear the
truth about the colonization of Hawaii and the betrayal
and overthrow of its Queen.

LYDIA AHOLO
(Cutting in)
Dr. Bateman, I am not interested in politics.
(Smiling)
That was always a source of contention between myself
and the Queen. She wanted me to distinguish myself as
a historian. That's why she sent me to college. But that
was her dream, not mine. All I wanted to do was to
return to Hawai'i, to my old boarding school, and to live
and work with my former teacher, Miss Ida Pope. That
was my dream, because, you see, she loved me. I was
Miss Pope's companion and secretary until she died. It
was a wonderful life.
(Pausing)
But the Queen could not understand it. She could not
understand how I could choose to be a secretary, for
twenty dollars a week—and room and board—when I
could have lived as the Queen's daughter in her
beautiful royal palace.
(Smiling)

LYDIA AHOLO (cont'd)
You know, the Queen even offered to pay me twenty
dollars a week, if I would leave Ida and come back and
live with her.

DR. BATEMAN
So why *have* you agreed to this interview?

LYDIA AHOLO
Because I need your help in answering the Queen's
question.

DR. BATEMAN
"The Queen's question?"

LYDIA AHOLO
The last year before she died, when she was telling me
the story of her life, there was a question that kept
tormenting her. She would ask it over and over.
     (She closes her eyes, remembering.)
"What did I do that was so wrong that I should lose my
country for my dear people?"
     (She opens her eyes.)
And then she turn to me and say, "Find out the answer,
Lydia, and tell the people."

DR. BATEMAN
     (Smiling)
But she didn't do anything wrong.

LYDIA AHOLO
     (Smiling back)
"What did I do that was so wrong that I should lose my
country for my dear people?"

147

DR. BATEMAN

There was nothing she could have done to save Hawai'i.
It was lost before she ever came to the throne—before
she was ever born. Your country was lost the day
Captain Cook sailed into Kealakekua Bay, in 1778.
There was nothing Queen Liliuokalani could have done
to save it.

LYDIA AHOLO

This was the Queen's last request of me, Dr. Bateman—
to answer her question, and it is my *aloha* to do that.
This is the reason why I have been willing to answer
your questions for these many months. Now I need to
ask you to help me answer the Queen's question.

DR. BATEMAN

(Patronizing her)
Miss Aholo...We have—what?—thirty tapes here?
That's sixty hours of oral history. And every reel of it
tells a tale of conspiracy and betrayal. Your own words!
There's nothing in here that answers that question.

LYDIA AHOLO

But it is my *aloha.*

DR. BATEMAN

(Angry)
How can it be an act of love to answer that question?

LYDIA AHOLO

(Angry)
Aloha is not "love!" Your language has no word for
aloha. What you call "love" is all about property, about
possession! This is why you have no balance—no *pono.*
　　　(DR. BATEMAN turns on the tape recorder.
　　　LYDIA AHOLO stops.)

DR. BATEMAN
(Looking up)
"Pono?"

LYDIA AHOLO
(After a pause)
We are an island people, Dr. Bateman, and on an island,
pono—balance—is vital to life. We have no new lands
to invade if we spoil what is ours. We must give back
what we take. We understand that it is dangerous to
make a profit from exchange. Our power depends on
pono, not conquest. Everything must be allowed to
flow—the language, the people, the wealth. This is why
we had no written word, no marriage, no money before
the *haoles*, the white foreigners, came. Everything was
free to flow, everything was sacred, everything was
aloha – the giving and giving-back of gifts. This is what
the Queen referred to as the "genius of a tropical
people."

DR. BATEMAN
I understand your *aloha*. I have my own sense of
obligation to "give back" for what I have received. Do
you want to know what it is?
(LYDIA waits.)
I am a white woman, a Western academic. I am part of
the culture that has destroyed yours. I'm not proud of
that, but I am dedicated to using the privilege I have
to…

LYDIA AHOLO
Get a book published.

DR. BATEMAN
(Switching off the tape recorder)

DR. BATEMAN (cont'd)
Yes, I will get a book published. It will be based on your
memoirs. But it's a book that will be challenged by
every historian in the country. It's not going to make me
any friends in academia, believe me. And I am going to
have to document every single detail ten times more
scrupulously than the academics who have built their
careers perpetuating the colonial, racist lies about your
country, and especially about your Queen. But you're
right. It's more than a political passion. It's a personal
crusade. You went to Oberlin College in 1917. You
must know what I'm talking about. At that time, Oberlin
was one of the few colleges in the world to admit
women as students. You must have faced discrimination
as a woman…

LYDIA AHOLO
I never wanted to attend college. That was the Queen's
idea.

DR. BATEMAN
(Starting again)
I faced discrimination. I wanted a doctoral degree in
history. At the time when I was in school, there were
very few women who got that far. Some dropped out to
get married and help their husbands or have babies.
Those of us who stayed were punished, because we
didn't do those things. I had to rewrite my dissertation
three times, and each time it was better than the
dissertations submitted by my male peers. I made a
vow – and this was my aloha—that if I ever received my
doctorate, I would dedicate my life work to uncovering
the history of women who had been buried by these
men. To write the first history of Queen Liliuokalani
that does not call her an ignorant savage, the first history
that does not attribute the colonization of Hawai'i to her

150

DR. BATEMAN (cont'd)
so-called misrule—that is my "aloha," my giving-back,
for the privilege I have as a white woman. And because
of *my* "aloha," I cannot answer the Queen's question. It
would be to betray everything I've worked for.
    (There is a long silence. LYDIA says nothing.
    DR. BATEMAN sighs and begins to collect the
    tapes.)
It seems that you aren't interested in finishing the
interview...I'm sorry, because we were almost through.
    (Pausing)
I wish we didn't have to end like this. I have really
enjoyed the time we spent working together—
    (She picks up the box of tapes.)

LYDIA AHOLO
    (Cutting her off)
Dr. Bateman.
    (DR. BATEMAN turns.)
Leave the tapes here.

DR. BATEMAN
What?

LYDIA AHOLO
Leave the tapes here.
    (Pausing)
They're not yours.

DR. BATEMAN
I'm sorry. I don't understand.

LYDIA AHOLO
They're not yours. Unless you are willing to help me
answer the Queen's question, I must ask you to leave
them here.

DR. BATEMAN

You don't mean that—

LYDIA AHOLO

This is your *aloha* to me.

DR. BATEMAN

(Becoming very formal)
No. This is not "aloha." You agreed to let me tape your
memoirs, and in return I agreed that I would let you
approve the manuscript. That was our agreement.

LYDIA AHOLO

Do you have it in writing?

DR. BATEMAN

I didn't think I needed to!

LYDIA AHOLO

That was very primitive of you.
(DR. BATEMAN cannot believe what she's
hearing. LYDIA smiles.)
"What did I do that was so wrong that I should lose my
country for my dear people?"
(There is a long pause. DR. BATEMAN, sets
the tapes down.)

DR. BATEMAN

All right. What did Queen Liliuokalani do that was so
wrong?
(LYDIA smiles. DR. BATEMAN is irritated.)
She asked that question. She tried to take responsibility
for everything that happened to her and to her people.
Like many women, she blamed herself for her
victimization.

LYDIA AHOLO
But that would not have caused her to lose the country.

DR. BATEMAN
(Exasperated)
All right. Where do you want to start?

LYDIA AHOLO
With the constitution.

DR. BATEMAN
Which one? You know there were several... The
Bayonet Constitution? The one her brother had been
forced to sign? The one that had already made it illegal
for Natives to vote before she even came to the throne?

LYDIA AHOLO
No, not the Bayonet Constitution.

DR. BATEMAN
Then you mean the one that she wrote herself, to restore
the voting rights?

LYDIA AHOLO
Yes, that one.

DR. BATEMAN
What about it?

LYDIA AHOLO
I want to hear what you have written about it.

DR. BATEMAN
Well, let me see...
(Shuffling through her notes)

DR. BATEMAN (cont'd)
That would have been in January of 1893...A year after
she had become queen...
(She's found it.)
Do you want the morning she called her Cabinet in to
sign it?

LYDIA AHOLO
Yes. Tell me exactly what she did that morning.

DR. BATEMAN
Well, according to your tapes, she had asked the
members of the Cabinet to meet with her at ten o'clock
at the palace in order to sign the new constitution into
law.

LYDIA AHOLO
And they came to the palace.

DR. BATEMAN
Yes, but they wouldn't sign it.
(Reading her notes)
They told her they hadn't read it.

LYDIA AHOLO
But they had. She had given them each a copy two
weeks earlier.

DR. BATEMAN
They lied. I told you—or, rather, you told me—they all
lied.
(Looking up)
She couldn't have done anything.

LYDIA AHOLO
She could have called for their resignation.

DR. BATEMAN

Yes, she could have done that. And then she would have needed to replace them, because, according to Article 78 of the Bayonet Constitution, she needed Cabinet approval for all her official acts. And the government, which was all *haoles*, was never going to approve a Cabinet sympathetic to the interests of the Native population.

LYDIA AHOLO

And so she had the new constitution read out loud to the Cabinet, and then she commanded them to do their duty and sign it.

DR. BATEMAN

And they refused again—this time, because, they said, there were too many problems with it.

LYDIA AHOLO

They made her look like a fool.

DR. BATEMAN

(Reading her notes)

"Thousands of Hawai'ians had gathered on the palace grounds to hear her proclaim the new constitution, and the throne room was packed with foreign diplomats who had been invited to witness the ceremonies."

(Looking up)

LYDIA AHOLO

They had encouraged her to do this. She said they had led her to the edge of a cliff and abandoned her. This was what she did wrong. She had believed her enemies.

DR. BATEMAN

But it didn't matter. Under the Bayonet Constitution, the monarch had no power and the Natives couldn't vote. The country was already lost.

LYDIA AHOLO

What do you have next in your writing?

DR. BATEMAN

She went out on the balcony and spoke to the people in Hawaiian. She asked them to go home quietly, and promised that, in a future time, she would proclaim a new constitution.

LYDIA AHOLO

That was it...the thing she did wrong.
    (DR. BATEMAN looks at her.)
That speech gave the *haoles* the excuse they needed. They said it was a call for revolution.

DR. BATEMAN

If she had not made that speech and that promise, there would have been rioting, and they would have accused her anyway. There was *nothing* she could have done.

LYDIA AHOLO

    (Angry)
She could have had them all arrested for treason!

DR. BATEMAN

Who? The men plotting against her were some of the highest-ranking members of the government. If she had issued warrants for their arrest, it would have been exactly the "proof" they were looking for.

LYDIA AHOLO

The people believed her. They would have supported her.

DR. BATEMAN

And that would have been considered an illegal uprising, and no government in the world would have been able to support it. Your people would have all been massacred.

LYDIA AHOLO

And so your government landed the Marines, and she abdicated.

DR. BATEMAN

They say she did.

LYDIA AHOLO

Do you have the document?

DR. BATEMAN

I think so.
    (Searching)
Here…
    (She hands it to LYDIA.)

LYDIA AHOLO

Read it.

DR. BATEMAN

    (Reading)
"I, Liliuokalani, by the Grace of God and under the Constitution of the Kingdom, Queen, do hereby solemnly protest against any and all acts done against myself and the constitutional Government of the

DR. BATEMAN (cont'd)
Hawai'ian Kingdom by certain persons claiming to have
established a provisional government of and for this
Kingdom.

"That I yield to the superior force of the United States of
America, whose minister plenipotentiary, His
Excellency John L. Stevens, has caused United States
troops to be landed at Honolulu and declared that he
would support the said provisional government. Now, to
avoid any collision of armed forces and perhaps the loss
of life, I do under this protest, and impelled by said
force, yield my authority until such time as the
Government of the United States shall, upon the facts
being presented to it, undo the action of its
representatives and reinstate me in the authority which I
claim as the constitutional sovereign of the Hawai'ian
Islands."

LYDIA AHOLO
She didn't abdicate.

DR. BATEMAN
No, but they said she did. They're still saying she did.
  (A pause)
There was nothing that your...your *hanai* could have
done to stop the overthrow. And there was nothing that
anyone could have done to stop the annexation. And
there was nothing that anyone could have done to stop
Hawai'i from becoming a state. Nothing.
  (She pauses, moving her chair closer to LYDIA.
  She takes the old woman's hands.)
And there's absolutely nothing anyone can do now to
give the land back to your people.
  (LYDIA pulls back her hands violently.

DR. BATEMAN (cont'd)
DR. BATEMAN feels she has made her point.)
It's too late. Nobody can change history.

LYDIA AHOLO

(Looking at her)
Except the *haoles.*

DR. BATEMAN

(Carefully)
No...They could write lies about it, or, like me, they can
attempt to correct those lies—but *nobody* can change
history. Not even me.

LYDIA AHOLO

Your words! Your *haole* words! We had no written
language before the missionaries came. They taught us
that this was because we were too primitive, but it was
you, the white foreigners—you!—the *haoles*—who were
too primitive. Our language was not written, because it
was too sophisticated, too subtle, to be reduced to
symbols on the page. It was a living language, like my
country, constantly in motion, constantly changing—
like a great river into which everything flowed. It was a
spiritual language that celebrated in exquisite detail the
great beauty of our land and our relationship to it. It was
a language of giving and giving back again—*aloha*—
reciprocation. But your language, the *haole* language, is
a dam. It stops the flow. Your language is not about life,
but about property. You take words and imprison them
on paper. You kill them and say you have rescued them;
you reduce them to the lowest common denominator and
then you say you have civilized them. You put them in a
dictionary and call this democracy, where the words
have no more voice, no more life. You kill them and
when they are dead and cannot speak for themselves,

LYDIA AHOLO (cont'd)
you name them law, and then you worship them like
gods. And you make written records of your conquests,
and this you call history, and you declare it sacred,
because you have no other heritage, no other legitimate
claim to the lands you have stolen.

DR. BATEMAN
(After a pause)
You would have agreed with the priestesses then.

LYDIA AHOLO

What priestesses?

DR. BATEMAN
The ones that came to the Queen after her abdication—
the women who tried to convince her to go back to the
old ways.

LYDIA AHOLO
I don't know this story. Where did you find it?

DR. BATEMAN
It was in the Queen's papers. She, of course, sent the
women away.

LYDIA AHOLO
Who were they? What did they want?

DR. BATEMAN
(Shuffling through her papers)
Let me see... That would have been 1893... Here it is...
(Reading)
It was after the abdication, but before she was arrested...

LYDIA AHOLO

Wait!
> (DR. BATEMAN looks at her.)

Turn on the tape.
> (DR. BATEMAN looks at her. After a pause,
> she turns it on. LYDIA watches her carefully.)

DR. BATEMAN

> (Reading)

"The United States had already landed the Marines, and
they were occupying the palace. In response to this,
there had been a great gathering of Native spiritual
leaders—"

LYDIA AHOLO

Kahunas.

DR. BATEMAN

Kahunas.
> (Reading)

"They had come from all the islands. They were
gathering because they had begun to feel that it was a
mistake to worship the god of the missionaries. They felt
that the christian god was only working in the interests
of the settlers, and that they needed to go back to
worshiping their own Native gods and goddesses. Three
of the older, more powerful women from this gathering
went to visit the Queen with a proposal: They wanted
her to join them in a ritual procession to Iolani Palace.
They would walk past the guards and the soldiers,
through the gate, and into the throne room—the three
kahunas in front, the Queen behind. Once inside the
throne room, they would lead the Queen to the throne,
and seat her on it."

LYDIA AHOLO

They would have been shot.

DR. BATEMAN

They knew that. It seems that was part of the plan.

LYDIA AHOLO

I don't understand.

DR. BATEMAN

It was going to be a sacrifice, a human sacrifice to one
of their gods—to Pele.

LYDIA AHOLO

The volcano goddess.

DR. BATEMAN

Yes, and the sacrifice would be accepted by her, because
the whole time they were marching past the guards and
up to the throne they would be performing some kind of
chant to her...

LYDIA AHOLO

(Startled)
The Pele Chant!

DR. BATEMAN

You know it?

LYDIA AHOLO

(Awed)
They were going to perform the Pele Chant...

DR. BATEMAN

What is it?

LYDIA AHOLO

The Pele Chant was very, very sacred. Only the very great *kahunas* were ever taught it. It's long, and quite complicated. All of the words have multiple meanings, and only a few *kahunas* are ever instructed in all the different meanings.
 (To herself)
So these women still knew the Pele Chant...

DR. BATEMAN

What was its purpose?

LYDIA AHOLO

The Pele Chant...

DR. BATEMAN

 (Pushing the tape recorder closer)
What was it used for?

LYDIA AHOLO

The Pele Chant invoked the names of our many ancestors, tracing their descent from the gods, and it was very important to remember all of these names precisely, because it would displease the gods to make any mistakes in our genealogy. This is because the gods live through us, and because we are held in proper relation to the land and to each other—not by law—but by our genealogy, by our earth mother, *Papa-hānau-moku*— "she who births the islands." It is very, very dangerous, when one is performing the Pele Chant, to take a breath or to hesitate in the wrong place, to mispronounce or to forget any of the long names. Performing the Pele Chant correctly required intense concentration, great clarity, and an absolute consecration of the spirit. This was a very dangerous thing these women were proposing to the Queen—to attempt the Pele Chant.

DR. BATEMAN

It was a very dangerous thing to enter an occupied palace.

LYDIA AHOLO

Which is more dangerous—to offend the goddess or to offend men?

DR. BATEMAN

Apparently, the Queen apparently decided it was more dangerous to offend men. She sent the women away. In fact, she was embarrassed by the incident, which is probably why she never told you about it.

LYDIA AHOLO

Oh, no, no, no... The Pele Chant...To perform it correctly, is not an *act* of liberation. It is to put oneself in the very state of liberation itself.

DR. BATEMAN

But they would have been shot...

LYDIA AHOLO

(Musing)

If the Queen had seated herself on the throne and then been physically forced off it by American soldiers, there would have been no question as to whether or not she abdicated. There would have been no confusion about your government's immoral use of armed force. If the soldiers had executed the *kahunas*—three unarmed, old women—all the world would have recognized the barbarity of your government's actions in invading a peaceful country and overthrowing its constitutional monarchy. My people would have risen, and every government in the world would have supported their

LYDIA AHOLO (cont'd)
cause, and your president would have been forced to
recognize the sovereignty of the Hawai'ian people.

DR. BATEMAN
(Shaking her head)
If the Queen had gone along with these *kahunas* and
their Pele Chant, she would have reinforced every
colonial stereotype about Native people—that they are
pagan, savage, ignorant, superstitious—

LYDIA AHOLO
(Excited, she ignores DR. BATEMAN.)
That was her mistake! She sent them away! She sent the
women away! That was what she did that was so wrong
it caused her to lose her country for her dear people!
That is the answer to the Queen's question! She sent the
women away!
(DR. BATEMAN looks at her in astonishment.)

DR. BATEMAN
You can't really believe that.

LYDIA AHOLO
(She stops the tape recorder and removes the
tape, holding it in her hand. She looks up at
DR. BATEMAN.)
I ka olelo ke ola. I ka olelo ka make.
(Pausing)
"In language is life. In language is death."

DR. BATEMAN
We say, "History is written by the conquerors."

165

LYDIA AHOLO
(Smiling)
That is not the same thing. You may have your tapes
now...
(She indicates the box on the floor. Slowly,
DR. BATEMAN reaches to pick it up.)
Except this tape. This tape is mine. This is my *aloha* to
the Queen. This is the answer to her question.
(She places the tape below the photograph of the
Queen.)

DR. BATEMAN
(Turning back at the door)
I'll send you a copy of the transcript.

LYDIA AHOLO
(Smiling)
They say Pele sometimes appears in human form before
there is an eruption...They say she appears as an old
woman.

(BLACKOUT)

THE END

Louisa May Incest

A One-Act Play for Two Women

Play Summary

Louisa May Alcott has locked her alter-ego, Jo March, out of her study in order to finish *Little Women* alone. Jo manages to break in. She confronts Louisa about her desire to end their collaboration. Louisa admits her intention to have Jo burn all her writing and marry the aging and self-righteous Professor Bhaer at the end of the book.

Jo knows her author better than Louisa knows herself, and she begins to uncover Louisa's true motives in violating her own creation. When Jo introduces evidence of Bronson Alcott's child molesting and Louisa's lesbianism, the conflict between Jo and Louisa becomes a life-and-death struggle for control of the book.

Two women
Thirty minutes
Single set

Cast of Characters

<u>Louisa May Alcott</u>: A woman of thirty-five.

<u>Jo March</u>: A woman in her early twenties with short
  hair.

Scene
Louisa May Alcott's room in Orchard House, Concord,
Massachusetts.

Time
1868.

Louisa May Incest

Setting: The scene is Louisa May
                    Alcott's room in Orchard
                    House, Concord, 1868.
                    Her father, Bronson
                    Alcott, is in his study
                    across the hall. LOUISA
                    is thirty-five years old.

At rise: LOUISA sits at her desk
                    and begins to write.
                    Uneasy, she rises and
                    crosses to the window.
                    She closes the curtains and
                    crosses to the door to lock
                    it. Returning to her desk,
                    she sits down and begins
                    to write again.

                    Someone is heard trying
                    the door handle. LOUISA
                    pretends to ignore the
                    intrusion. Finding it
                    locked, the outsider tries
                    to force the lock. Then she
                    knocks. Finally she calls
                    out.

                            JO
    (Offstage)
Louisa! Louisa! I can't get in! The door must be locked.
    (LOUISA looks up from her work, disturbed, but
    she resolves to ignore the voice. She continues to
    write.)
Louisa! Can you hear me? Louisa! It's me, Jo!

JO (cont'd)

(She rattles the knob.)

Louisa! I can hear you…. What's the matter? Is someone else there? Louisa? Are you all right? Louisa, answer me! I'm going to break the door down.

(JO begins to batter the door. LOUISA, frightened, sits frozen at her desk.)

Don't worry, Louisa, I'm coming….

(Suddenly the door gives, and JO rushes in.

JO is JO MARCH from *Little Women*. She is   in her early twenties, with very short hair. Jo   trips, landing at Louisa's feet.)

Louisa! Louisa, are you all right?

(She throws her arms around the older woman.)

What's the matter, dearest? Why was the door locked?

(LOUISA looks away.)

Oh, Louisa, you weren't thinking those glum thoughts again, were you? Why didn't you call for me earlier? Is it your family again? It was Bronson, wasn't it? I saw the light on in his study across the hall. It was your father, wasn't it? He's been criticizing you again, hasn't he?

LOUISA

No. It has nothing to do with my family.

JO

What is it, darling? You know I'd do anything in the world for you. Is it one of your publishers? I know a thing or two about those men. It is, isn't it?

LOUISA

No, it's not.

JO

(She sees the manuscript out on the table.)

JO (cont'd)

It's *Little Women*, then, isn't it? You're depressed about
how it's going...Well, of course you are! You've been
pegging away at it for months, day and night. Of course,
you're tired... After all, you're *human*. Me, I could just
rattle along forever, telling stories and blundering
through...But, of course, it's not the same for you. You
need to eat and sleep! I've been so *thoughtless*.... It's all
my fault! Whenever you want to work, I just get so
excited about the book, I get started, and I don't know
when to stop... You see—I'm doing it now! You just
turn and say, "Jo March, that's enough now," and I'll
stop right where I am! Oh, I can see now that you
haven't been taking enough time to rest... And you
haven't eaten yet, have you? and it's nearly four—

LOUISA

It isn't me. I'm fine.

JO

Well, you dear...of course you'd say that if a ton of
bricks fell on your head. That's just what I would say
too, so I know. But you can't fool me, Louisa May
Alcott! You can't fool your Jo! You've been working
too hard...

LOUISA

No, I haven't.

JO

...*but* you think your family needs the money, so you're
racing to finish the book! That's exactly what I would
do—but it isn't right! You deserve a rest... We'll work
on this tomorrow. Today, you just take a walk out in the
sunshine, and eat a big healthy dinner...and I don't care
what your father says, a little red meat wouldn't do you

JO (cont'd)

any harm...and you go to bed early—no reading! And tomorrow, bright and early, when you come into the study, I'll be waiting for you, and we'll start right in... You'll see! We'll work so hard tomorrow, because we'll be fresh, that we'll get twice as much done—and you won't have lost any work from today. Now, go on... Get your hat ... Go on! I'll be waiting here...

LOUISA

I'm not tired. And I don't want to go out. And I don't want you to wait here.

(JO is surprised by the sharpness in her voice.)
I want to finish the book without you.

JO

(After a long pause)
You mean I'm going to die like Beth?

LOUISA

(Avoiding her eyes)
You're not going to die. You're the main character.

JO

Then I don't understand. I thought we were writing this together.

LOUISA

We were. But I need to finish it alone.

JO

It's my dreadful language, isn't it... all that slang? "Christopher Columbus" and—

LOUISA

No, it's not the slang.

JO

Yes, it is! I know... and my selfishness...

LOUISA

(Smiling)
You're not selfish, Jo.

JO

Oh, yes, I am! I'm not at all generous like Marmee, or Beth...and I've never learned to cook like Meg, and I'm not the least bit artistic like Amy...

LOUISA

You're fine, Jo.

JO

No, I'm not a bit. And I don't blame you at all for wanting to work without me. There! That's what I deserve for being so vain about my writing! And all I've published is a few stories in the *Weekly Volcano*. And here I've been thinking I can write a real book with a real author... Well, I don't blame you a bit, Louisa! And I'm grateful you let me work with you as long as you did—although, of course, I should have seen it couldn't last... Well, there! That's enough of that, Josephine March! Now you just stop feeling sorry for yourself and get back to your own work!
(She rises.)

LOUISA

Jo, wait.
(JO turns.)
Come back.

JO

I don't want to keep your from your writing.

LOUISA

There's plenty of time for that. Come here.
     (JO returns to her side.)
Oh, Jo, I'm going to miss you.
     (She hugs her.)

JO

(Rallying)
Well, it's not like I'll be gone forever... I'll come back
when the book is finished, and you can tell me all about
it, and we'll celebrate... And maybe, by then, I will have
published something of my own—and you can be proud
of me...

LOUISA

I *am* proud of you.

JO

Oh, Louisa, I don't deserve it, but I do so much love it
when you say things like that.
     (She sits at her feet.)

LOUISA

(Reaching down and rumpling her hair)
Look at this hair...

JO

It's growing back!

LOUISA

I like it short.

176

                    JO
So do I.
          (She catches LOUISA's hand.)
Is your hand still cramped?

                 LOUISA
It's not too sore today.

                    JO
Let me work on it.
          (She massages LOUISA's hand.)
How does that feel?

                 LOUISA
Better.

                    JO
I could still come every day and work on your hand. I
could help you that way...

                 LOUISA
No.

                    JO
Why? I know I'm not as good a writer as you, but I
could still help you in other ways... And I can be very
quiet... Really...

                 LOUISA
Dear Jo... I won't be able to finish the book if you're
here.

                    JO
Why not?

LOUISA

Because it's time for you to start growing up.

JO

(Getting up quickly from the floor and sitting
in a chair)

I *am* growing up. I just forget sometimes.

LOUISA

I'm not talking about your sitting on the floor.

JO

(Looking down)

I know what you're talking about.

LOUISA

You do?

JO

Of course... I think about it all the time when I'm by
myself.

(LOUISA looks alarmed.)

I know you're disappointed in my writing. So am I..

(LOUISA relaxes.)

I haven't been working on it nearly as much as I
should... And mostly I've been trying to write those
stories that will sell. And I know you're thinking it's
time I took my work more seriously, if I'm to become a
successful writer by the end of the book. Here we are
three hundred pages along, and I still haven't done
anything...

LOUISA

(Looking away)

It's not your writing...

JO

Don't try to be tactful! I know! But now that I've moved
away from home to the rooming house, I'll be able to
work better. There won't be so many interruptions...

LOUISA

That's not what I meant when I said you needed to grow
up.

JO

I don't understand.

LOUISA

I need to make plans for your future.

JO

(Puzzled)
I'm going to be a writer like you.
(LOUISA says nothing.)
I thought that was obvious... It's right there on the very
first page about how much I love books... And then
there's that little collection of children's stories I've
written... And the Pickwick Club, and how I was the
editor of the Club's paper... *Everyone* has *always* known
that I would be a writer...
(She crosses her arms with determination.)
I'm going to write a great book someday and make lots
of money, just like you!

LOUISA

You need a family...

JO

I have a family—Amy, Meg—

LOUISA

(Cutting her off)
Meg is married.

JO

She's still my family!

LOUISA

(Smiling)
You never could accept losing her.

JO

(Defensive)
Just because she got married, she's still my sister!

LOUISA

Jo, you need a family of your own.

JO

(Sitting in silence for a minute)
Louisa, I thought you agreed that I wouldn't have to marry Laurie. You said that Amy was going to marry him.

LOUISA

She is.

JO

Then what are you talking about? You're two thirds the way through the book and there isn't anybody else for me to marry—unless it's Laurie's grandfather, old Mr. Laurence!

LOUISA

It's not Mr. Laurence.

JO

Well, then it's too late... You can't introduce a new
character this late in the book. Your readers would never
believe it. I'm just going to stay in my rooming house
until I sell my first book...and then I'm going to buy a
house big enough for Marmee and Amy and—

LOUISA

There *is* someone else.
          (JO looks at her.)
Someone in the rooming house.

JO

          (She is confused for a moment until she realizes
          what LOUISA has in mind.)
You're not serious...! Louisa!
          (LOUISA looks away.)
That seedy German professor? Louisa!

LOUISA

You like him.

JO

I like him, but I'm not going to marry him. He's old
enough to be my father!

LOUISA

          (Alarmed about Bronson overhearing their
          conversation, she crosses to the door and closes
          it.)
This is what I mean about our not being able to work
together any more.

JO

Friedrich Bhaer is shabby, and repulsive, and bigoted,
and doesn't take care of himself, and he can hardly

181

JO (cont'd)

speak English!

LOUISA

He's German...

JO

And he has two children, two *boys*!

LOUISA

They're his nephews.

JO

But *he's* raising them!

LOUISA

He loves children.

JO

I can't believe you're serious about this. It must be some
kind of joke. Louisa—
        (LOUISA has turned away.)
Talk to me!

LOUISA

There's no point in discussing it if you're going to be
hysterical.

JO

        (Scared)
What have I done? I've been too wild...haven't I? I've
been too lazy... I'll do better! I'm going to sit myself
down and write for eight hours a day... See if I don't!
        (Pleading with LOUISA)
Just give me one year at the rooming house! If by then I
haven't published a book, you can marry me off to

JO (cont'd)
anybody in the world, and I won't say a word... I
promise! Just give me a year!

LOUISA
Jo, it isn't a punishment! He's a good man...

JO
So is Laurie, but I don't have to marry him!

LOUISA
Laurie is a boy... The Professor is a man.

JO

An *old* man.

LOUISA
A *mature* man. You need someone mature.

JO

Why?

LOUISA
Because you lack moral judgment.

JO

(Angry)
What does that mean?

LOUISA
You don't always do the right thing. You go by your
feelings too much.

JO
I don't feel like marrying that seedy, self-righteous
bigot!

LOUISA

I'm not surprised. Feelings are usually selfish.

JO

(Shouting)

That's not selfish! How would you like to marry him?
(LOUISA turns back to her papers, ignoring JO.
JO struggles to regain control of her feelings.)
I'm sorry.
(She sits.)

LOUISA

(Looking up)

I've chosen Professor Bhaer because of his maturity. He
has the wisdom to help you become the woman you
want to be.

JO

How is he going to do that? Teach me German?
(LOUISA turns away again.)
I'm sorry, Louisa. How is he going to help me?

LOUISA

He is going to keep you aware of what is really
important in life.

JO

And what is really important in life?

LOUISA

Serving others.

JO

(Exploding)

I do! That's all I've ever done! This move to the

JO (cont'd)
rooming house is the first time I've ever even begun to
have a life of my own! And this money I've begun to
earn for writing stories—this is the first time I've ever
had a taste of being independent!

LOUISA
I don't think the rooming house was a good idea. I'm
afraid that when I wrote that chapter, I was a little
carried away by your ideas.

JO
What are you talking about?

LOUISA
Those stories you write.

JO
What about them?

LOUISA
Are you proud of them?

JO
(Defensively)
I'm proud of the money.

LOUISA
(Looking away)
This is why you need Professor Bhaer.

JO
What's he got to do with my writing?

LOUISA
He's going to make you see what you're doing to

185

LOUISA (cont'd)

yourself by writing those trashy stories for money.

JO

He can't do that.

LOUISA

(Smiling)
He already has.

JO

(Suddenly understanding what LOUISA is
saying)
You've written it! You've written it in without me!
(JO grabs the papers from LOUISA's desk
and begins to read.)
"I would more rather give my boys gun-powder to play
with than this bad trash..."! That moralizing, pompous,
conceited, jackass! He doesn't have a family of six to
support! How dare he—

LOUISA

(Rising, flushed)
Give them back!

JO

(Continuing to read)
"If respectable people knew what harm they did, they
would not feel then the living was honest." How dare he
say that to me? Does he have any idea what I would
have to be doing if I wasn't writing these stories? Does
he have the faintest idea of how hard it is for a woman to
make money? Has he ever been a live-in companion—to
put up with the sexual advances of every male in the
household? Do know what things I would be doing if I
were a man? Do you know what I would do if I could

186

JO (cont'd)
have gone to college and gotten a degree? You can
believe I wouldn't be living in some broken-down
rooming house, giving German lessons for a living!
Louisa—think of it! Think what we would be doing if
we had been allowed to go to college!

LOUISA
You're wrong about Professor Bhaer. He's a great man.
Now, give those back.

JO
      (Reading again)
"Jo. ...stuffed the whole bundle into her stove..."
      (She looks up.)
I *burn* my writing?
      (LOUISA tries to snatch the papers, but JO
      dodges her.)
I *burn* my own writing, because of what this self-
righteous lecher says?

LOUISA
      (She finally succeeds in retrieving the papers.)
This is why it's impossible for us to collaborate!

JO
I can't believe it... I *burn* my own writing?

LOUISA
Yes.
      (Avoiding her eyes)
Like the way you cut off your hair.

JO
It's not the same thing.

LOUISA

Yes, it is. It's for a higher principle.

JO

No, it isn't. Hair grows back. Don't you remember how
I wouldn't even speak to Amy when she got mad at me
and burned that little book of stories? You had to almost
drown her to make me feel like forgiving her.
Remember? And now you're going to expect me to take
my own writings—writings that pay the rent!—and *burn*
them? I wouldn't do it.

LOUISA

You *will* do it. I've written it.

JO

No, I won't. I won't do it. You can write it, but I won't
be there... and all your readers will know!

LOUISA

You'll do it, because it's the right thing to do.

JO

What about you? Would you burn your own writing?
Would you burn *Little Women*?

LOUISA

I don't need to. It's a children's story. It isn't trash.

JO

What about your romance stories?

LOUISA

I don't have any.

JO

Don't lie to me! I know you. Where do you think I stole
my plots from?

LOUISA

I don't know what you're talking about.

JO

(Angry)
Oh, don't you… "Flora Fairfield...?" "A. M.
Barnard...?"
(LOUISA freezes.)
Those are your pen names, aren't they...? The ones you
used when you wrote "The Rival Painters?"..."The
Abbot's Ghost?"..."Pauline's Passion?"

LOUISA

Where did you find those?

JO

I didn't need to find them. They're in your head. I know
you better than you know me.

LOUISA

I have had to support a real family. Yours is make-
believe. It's different.

JO

How?

LOUISA

How? All I have to do is write a sentence, and suddenly
you've sold a story! It's not that easy for me. I have to
write it. I have to send it out. It gets returned; it gets lost;
nobody buys it... That's real life, Jo! That's *my* life! You
should thank me that I have decided you don't have to

LOUISA (cont'd)

struggle the way I have. I'm going to have your Aunt March die and leave you her estate. Nobody is going to do that for me! Nobody's going to write a happy ending for me!

JO

Maybe I don't want a happy ending. Maybe I choose to write, because I love it. Maybe I'm just like you.

LOUISA

(Bitterly)
I write for the money.

JO

Don't lie to me... You write those thriller stories for the same reason I do—because you like to! You get to say all kinds of unladylike things... You get to kill men... You get to pretend you're a man and write about laying your head against a woman's breast—

LOUISA

(Agitated)
Jo! What are you talking about?

JO

I'm talking about you—about us! You wish you could live like a man just as much as I do.

LOUISA

No, I don't.

JO

Where do you think I get my ideas from? You call me "fellow," you cut all my hair off, you call me the man of the family. I use slang, I race Laurie and beat him, I give

JO (cont'd)

my money to support the family, I'm wildly jealous of
John for marrying Meg... Louisa, you know what I am
as well as I do. That's why I can't get married.

LOUISA

You're a tomboy. You just need to grow up.

JO

Look again, Louisa. You need to grow up. I'm a lesbian.

LOUISA

No! No, you're not!

JO

Yes, I am. Remember what you had me tell Laurie—
"It's impossible for people to make themselves love
other people if they don't..." Remember? We told him,
"I don't believe it's the right sort of love, and I'd rather
not try it." You know why I said that.

LOUISA

Laurie was a friend, but I never intended those remarks
to refer to all men.

JO

Louisa, you know I love women. You know that! You
know because you created me out of your own need to
love women...

LOUISA

I don't want to love them like that!

JO

Oh yes, you do, Louisa May Alcott...and you want them
to love you like that.

191

LOUISA

No!

> JO crosses to LOUISA.
> She takes her hand, the
> writing hand, and caresses
> it. LOUISA closes her
> eyes. JO takes her hand
> and brings it to her lips.
> She begins to kiss and
> caress her fingers.

JO

Louisa, you are so beautiful... You take care of
everybody... Who takes care of you? Nobody sees you
like I do... I see who you are—I see how beautiful you
are... Let me love you, Louisa...
(She kisses her lips. LOUISA, after the kiss,
turns away in confusion.)

LOUISA

I was in love with David...

JO

Louisa...

LOUISA

I was! I would have married him...

JO

Henry David Thoreau despised women, and you know
it. He liked little boys.

LOUISA

I loved him...

JO

You loved him, because you knew you'd never have to do anything about it.

LOUISA

And I loved Ladislas...

JO

That *boy* you met three years ago in Switzerland?

LOUISA

I was in love with him.

JO

You were infatuated! He was eighteen...you were thirty-three... You were attracted to him, because he was the closest thing to a woman you could find.

LOUISA

(Turning to look at JO)
No! You're twisting things...

JO

Louisa, you're the one twisting things. Look at who you pick to fall in love with—homosexual men and adolescent boys!

LOUISA

(Rising)
No!

JO

Yes! The reason you have never married, is because you're a lesbian... Like me...
(She puts her arms around LOUISA.)

LOUISA

No! No...

JO

Louisa, I love you... I'm the only one who has *ever* loved you... That's what you created me for!

LOUISA

I created you for Professor Bhaer.

JO

You created me for your own pleasure.

LOUISA

(Pulling away)
No. I created you to marry him...

JO

(Nuzzling LOUISA's neck)
I can't do that, and you don't want me to.

LOUISA

Yes, yes I do... Jo, he's kind... He needs you...

JO

You need me.

LOUISA

(Desperate)
You'll inherit Plumfield! You won't have to write!

JO

I'm going to stay and work with you.
(She kisses LOUISA's lips.)

LOUISA

(Pulling away)
You *have* to marry him!

JO

Louisa! Think about what you're asking... Think of the wedding night!

LOUISA

I'm not going to write about that.

JO

But your readers are going to think about it... Think of his seedy trousers coming down! Think of that big, pink-grey penis coming out, sticking out like an elephant's trunk—

LOUISA

Stop it!

JO

Think about his bad breath in my face, his hairy stomach lying over my body! Think about his grunting, and sweating, and rocking back and forth! That's what marriage is about!

LOUISA

It's a union of two souls! It's a lifetime of companionship!

JO

It's him lying on top of me every night and shooting his sperm between my legs!

LOUISA

(Delirious)

LOUISA (cont'd)

I'm leaving!
>(She opens the door to exit.)

JO

Just because your father violated you, don't violate me!

LOUISA

>(Turning)

That's a lie!
>(She shuts the door quickly, so Bronson can't hear.)

JO

Oh, Louisa, come on!

LOUISA

My father is a good and pure and true man! He's one of the most highly evolved souls in Cambridge... Ask anyone here!

JO

You hate him.

LOUISA

I aspire to be like him.

JO

You hate him.

LOUISA

No, *you* hate him. You're jealous.

JO

I do hate him. I hate him for what he's done to you.

LOUISA

You don't know what you're talking about!

JO

Why do you think he lost all those schools?

LOUISA

Because his ideas on educating children were ahead of
his time.

JO

He lost the school in Cheshire because he invited the
children to his rooms after school, and he was caught
"caressing" the girls.

LOUISA

That's a lie.

JO

No, it isn't. Remember how he lost Temple School,
because he wanted to talk about sex to the children?

LOUISA

He was honest and uninhibited.

JO

Was that why he would spend hours in the bath with
you? Is that why he slept with you at night? Is that why
your mother was desperate to place you in another home
when you were two?

LOUISA

He was a loving father.

JO

What about that dream you keep having over and over?

JO (cont'd)

The nightmare with the man saying, "Lie still, my dear!"
The man who is always coming after you...the man who
threatens you all night long? Where do you think you
got that nightmare?

LOUISA

Dreams don't mean anything.

JO

And how about your father's writing? Have you ever
read his books? How about *Observations on the Life of
My Second Child, Louisa May Alcott, During the First
Year*? Have you read about his little experiments with
you and your sister? How your loving father would burn
Anna's hand to record her reaction? Or how he would
take her to the park and then hide, to see what she would
do? Do you really believe he didn't perform other kinds
of experiments?

LOUISA

I don't believe it.

JO

It's a fact.

LOUISA

How do you know?

JO

Because you know.

LOUISA

No, I don't.

JO

Yes, you do. You just won't open those parts of your mind. But I can see all of you, because I don't need to protect Bronson. In fact, I would like to kill him.

LOUISA

Jo! Don't say that! If anything happened to Father, I wouldn't be able to live!

JO

That's probably true, but we can change the ending, Louisa. I can help you expose your father and get him out of your life! Here...take these chapters you wrote without me... Professor Bhaer doesn't belong in our book. He's your father... Take these and burn them.

LOUISA

Now you expect me to burn *my* work.

JO

You didn't really write these. Bronson dictated them to you. Professor Bhaer is his alter-ego. Burn them. Burn them, Louisa, and we'll rewrite the ending where I meet a wonderful older woman who is a writer, and we write a book together, and it becomes a great success, and we buy a house, and we meet all the brightest women in Boston, and they come to our home every week for salons...forever and ever.

LOUISA

(Taking the chapters, she moves toward the fireplace)
I could be one of the boarders at the rooming house.

JO

You could. We could read to each other what we've
written every evening.

LOUISA

You would sleep with me...?

JO

(Cautiously)
Would you want me to?

LOUISA

(A long pause)
I see what's going on here... You are tempting me.
    (LOUISA begins to speak in a style of oratory
    she has picked up from her father.)
You, my creation, are the personification of all my
weaknesses. This is my selfishness, my self-indulgence,
my carnal desires speaking to me. I know you, Jo
March—you are my own worst self!

JO

Your *best* self, Louisa! You are talking like Bronson
now... He wants to ruin your life! He's taken thirty-five
years already. He's a vampire! He sucks your life blood,
and now he's sucking your creative blood. Don't let
him, Louisa! Burn these chapters.

LOUISA

(Becoming very distant and rhetorical)
Oh, you're clever, Jo March... I might have known you
would be. I was always able to fool myself... If it
weren't for the firm moral foundation my father laid in
me, I might be tempted to listen to you. But thankfully I
have his strong example to guide me. Without him, I
would steer like a ship without a rudder, giving in to my

LOUISA (cont'd)
impulses at every instant, headed nowhere at all and wrecking myself on the treacherous shoals of self-gratification.

JO
(She grabs LOUISA's shoulders.)
What are you talking about? Living your own life is not a crime!

LOUISA
You're a clever temptress.

JO
Louisa, your father is a child molester.

LOUISA
You must be very weak to malign such a good man.

JO
He is! You know it! Every sentence you write reeks of incest!

LOUISA
Poor Jo—your father was away, wasn't he, and you're jealous that I have always lived so close to mine... You can't understand what it is to have a saint for a father.

JO
A *saint*! Bronson Alcott is a *devil*!
(She grabs the chapters.)

LOUISA
(Gently)
You know you can't act without my permission. You are my creation.

JO

I know that deep down you want me to burn these. I
know that's what's in your heart.

> (She crosses to the fireplace. LOUISA watches
> her. JO picks up the matches and freezes.)

Louisa, please... I know you must want to be happy.

LOUISA

My father has taught me the way to happiness is self-
sacrifice.

JO

> (Frantic)

That's the way to *his* happiness. When have you ever
seen Bronson do anything for anybody else? Haven't
you and your mother been supporting him for twenty
years? What has he ever done for his family, except
molest and abandon you?

LOUISA

> (Not hearing her)

You see, you can't burn them. I don't want you to. You
will put them on my desk.

> (JO obeys.)

JO

This means I will have to burn my work. It's in this
chapter.

LOUISA

Yes, you will. It's the right thing.

JO

Oh, Louisa, you have killed us both.

LOUISA

Little Women will be a great success.

JO

Only in a world of incest.

LOUISA

I think you can go now.

JO

I'll never come back.

LOUISA

That's as it should be. The Professor will need you more
than I do.

JO

You and your book are poisoned!

LOUISA

(Smiling)
Oh, I forgot to tell you... You and the Professor are
going to turn Plumfield into a school for little boys.

JO turns to look at her a
final time. Silently she
exits, closing the door
behind her. LOUISA picks
up her manuscript.

(BLACKOUT)

THE END

The Rules of the Playground

A One-Act Play

Play Summary

Five women, all mothers, have gathered in a classroom of their children's middle school to take part in an experimental, new program designed to eliminate playground violence. Experts from international "think tanks" and peacekeeping forces are training the women on how to analyze playground dynamics in order to detect the class, ethnic, and racial inequalities among the children that are, in theory, the sources of conflict. The program's focus is emphatically on confronting social imbalances, not individual behaviors, and, to facilitate this focus, the women have been forbidden to look out the window at the playground. In fact, the blinds are shut.

An enthusiastic newcomer joins the group, but her enthusiasm changes to confusion as it is revealed that, a week earlier, one child was shot on the playground and another was raped. The newcomer reacts with disbelief and then alarm, as the sounds of gunfire and screaming are heard from the playground.

This is a scathing social satire, along the lines of Shirley Jackson's electrifying short story "The Lottery." *The Rules of the Playground* demonstrates how the everyday social conditioning of women is exploited in order to perpetuate denial and compliance.

Six women
Twenty-five minutes
Single set

Cast of Characters

<u>Madeleine</u>: A mother, 35-50.

<u>Jeanne:</u> A mother, 35-50.

<u>Margaret</u>: A mother, 35-50.

<u>Goldie</u>: A mother, 35-50.

<u>Indira</u>: A mother, 35-50.

<u>Shelley</u>: A mother, 35-50.

Scene
A classroom in a middle school.

Time
The present.

Ethnicity Chart

	MONDAY	TUESDAY	WEDNESDAY	THURSDAY	FRIDAY
BB HOOP	AA	AsA	PRA	MA/H	EA
MONKEY BARS	AsA	PRA	MA/H	EA	AA
SWINGS	PRA	MA/H	EA	AA	AsA
TREES	MA/H	EA	AA	AsA	PRA
PICNIC TABLES	EA	AA	AsA	PRA	MA/H

KEY:
AA-AFRICAN AMERICAN
AsA-ASIAN AMERICAN
EA-EUROPEAN AMERICAN
MA/H-MEXICAN AMERICAN/HISPANIC
PRA-PUERTO AMERICAN AMERICAN

MAP OF THE PLAYGROUND

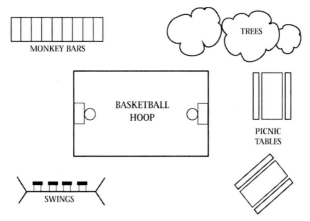

The Rules of the Playground

Setting:	The interior of a middle school classroom. There are rows of windows, with blinds or curtains, along the back wall. These windows look out over the playground. At the start of the play, all of the blinds have been pulled down, completely obscuring the view of the playground.
	Up left are two large easels. One displays the "Ethnicity Chart," and the other supports a large dryboard with the map of the playground. Downstage left is the doorway into the classroom from the hall. Down right is a small table with a coffeemaker, sugar, cups, etc. Rows of chairs, or chairs with desks are in the center of the stage, facing left.
At Rise:	The classroom is empty. MADELEINE enters carrying her copy of the "PDA Handbook." (All of the women except SHELLEY will have a

copy of this.)
MADELEINE is uneasy.
She sets her handbook on
one of the chairs and
crosses to the coffee pot.
She is pouring herself a
cup of coffee when
JEANNE enters. Startled,
MADELEINE spills her
coffee.

MADELEINE

(Distracted, as she tries to clean up the spill
using napkins)

Jeanne...

(JEANNE, who has crossed purposefully to one
of the chairs, is busy with her notebook and
purse.)

I... I didn't expect to see you here...

JEANNE

(All business)

Why not?

(MADELEINE does not know what to say.)

I think it's even more important for me to be here now.

MADELEINE

You're right. I wasn't thinking... Can I get you some
coffee?

JEANNE

No, thank you.

(She seats herself in the front row, facing the
easels.)

MADELEINE

(Fishing.)
It's certainly challenging to change the way we think
about things...

JEANNE

(Turning)
And how are *you* doing?

MADELEINE

Oh... I... Well... It's been a hard week... But not as hard
as yours.

JEANNE

(Sternly.)
There's no way to compare the two experiences.
     (Suddenly noticing the blinds/curtains)
Why are the blinds [curtains] up?

MADELEINE

(Panicked)
Oh! I didn't realize they were...

JEANNE

Did you look?

MADELEINE

(Backing up toward the window)
No... No, I haven't been near the window.
     (Closing the blinds/curtains without facing them)
It must have been from last week...when I heard
the...you know...when the...
     (She checks herself and lapses into silence.
There is a pause.)

JEANNE

How *is* your daughter?

MADELEINE

(Retreating to a seat at the back of the classroom)
Oh...well...we've both been working very hard. It hasn't
been easy, dislodging stereotypes.... Especially about
gender...

JEANNE

Yes.

MADELEINE

Really? You, too? I would have thought—

JEANNE

(Cutting her off.)
Of course.
(A beat)
Is she on the playground? Did you bring her?

MADELEINE

(Long pause.)
She's at home.
(JEANNE looks at her. MADELEINE is very
uncomfortable.)
I'm hoping she'll decide to come next week...
(Embarrassed)
I'd rather the others didn't know that she didn't come
today...

> Just then MARGARET
> enters with artificial
> briskness. She marches
> straight over to the coffee,
> pretending not to see

214

JEANNE. JEANNE and
MADELEINE have a
strong and immediate
response to her presence.
They look away from her.

MARGARET
(Greeting MADELEINE, who is sitting close to
the table)
Good morning.
(MADELEINE turns, but does not say anything.)
That was a wonderful workshop last week, wasn't it?
It's all about focus, isn't it? I just got so much out of
it—didn't you?
(MADELEINE turns away. MARGARET,
pretending to ignore this, turns to survey the
classroom.)
I wonder where the trainer is...?

JEANNE
It's early.

MARGARET
(Pretending to notice JEANNE for the first
time.)
Oh...Jeanne! What a surprise to see you!

JEANNE
(Not taken in by MARGARET's performance.)
And why is it a surprise?

MARGARET
(Attempting to patronize her.)
Well, really, there's no need for you to be here *now*.

JEANNE

(Rising)
I think there's very much a need..."*now.*"

MARGARET

Well, it *is* a workshop for *parents*.

MADELEINE

Jeanne is still a parent.

GOLDIE

(Just then GOLDIE enters with a plate of brownies
covered with plastic wrap. She gasps
when she sees JEANNE.)
Jeanne! I am so glad to see you!
(She crosses to hug her. JEANNE receives the
embrace with stiff formality.)
I wanted to call you, but I wasn't sure if it would be
okay...after what they said at the workshop about
"focus" and everything.... But here you are, and I'm so
glad to see you! How are you?
(JEANNE doesn't respond.)

MADELEINE

Jeanne feels it's important to finish the training.

GOLDIE

Well, good for you! And we're glad you're here!
(She hugs her again and then looks around.)
I made us some brownies for the workshop today. I
thought it might be nice to have a little something to
nibble on, along with our coffee.

MADELEINE

This isn't a tea party.

GOLDIE
(Crossing to the chair in front of MADELEINE)
Oh, my god! Oh, Madeleine! I am *so* sorry... I had
forgotten completely... I was just so glad to see Jeanne
here after what happened last week.... I totally forgot
about your Christy! How is she?

MADELEINE
We're working with it.

GOLDIE
Oh, bless her heart! I know she's being so brave. What a
little soldier! I certainly didn't mean any disrespect. If
you think it's inappropriate to have the brownies here, I
can just put them out in my car... It's not a problem at
all. They were just kind of a little spur-of-the moment
thing... I just really didn't think—

MARGARET
(Crossing aggressively to GOLDIE)
I'll have one.
(GOLDIE breaks off and turns to look at
MARGARET for the first time since she
entered.)
I didn't have any breakfast.
(There's an awkward pause. GOLDIE unwraps
a corner of the plate and holds the dish out to
MARGARET. MARGARET peels back the rest
of the plastic to survey all the brownies. She
takes two and bites into one.)
Mmm...delicious.

> MARGARET crosses
> back to the last row and
> sits by MADELEINE.
> GOLDIE turns

217

apologetically toward
JEANNE and
MADELEINE,
embarrassed to be feeding
the enemy. She places the
brownies on an empty
chair. Just then INDIRA
enters with SHELLEY.

INDIRA

(To SHELLEY)
Oh, good—we're still early.
(To the others)
Hello, ladies—I want you all to meet Shelley.
(They all turn to look at her.)
She's new to the district.

SHELLEY

I just moved here...

INDIRA

They told her she was too late to get into the program,
because she had already missed the first session, but
Shelley wouldn't take "no" for an answer, so here she is!
They asked me to do the introductions...

GOLDIE

Hi, Shelley. Welcome to the program. I'm Goldie.

MADELEINE

Madeleine.

MARGARET

(Sourly)
Margaret.
(A silence)

INDIRA

And this is Jeanne.

SHELLEY
(Oblivious to the tension in the room, SHELLEY
waxes enthusiastic)

Well, I just thought it was so wonderful to see a middle-
school so committed to eliminating violence—and not
just in a kind of window-dressing way—but to have
such a commitment that they bring this kind of program
in—I mean international peacekeeping experts from
some of the biggest think tanks in the country, coming
here—to a *middle school*—to analyze what's happening
on the playground like it was some kind of international
conflict... I mean to take it so *seriously*, what happens
with children, as if the world depended on it—which it
does, because *this* is where it all starts...right here... I
mean, this is just so *radical*! And *then*, to focus on the
mothers for the training... It's just so *refreshing* to see a
program that acknowledges the fact that we *are* the
primary caregivers and that our influence is really
unique. I just really appreciate that, because I'm a single
mother.
(She pauses.)
Is anyone else here a single mom?

GOLDIE
(Eager to redeem herself)

Jeanne—
(There is an awkward silence. GOLDIE, with
horror, realizes her mistake.)

JEANNE
(Turning around)

I *was* a single mother. My son is dead.

SHELLEY

Oh, I'm sorry.

JEANNE

My son died as a result of playground violence, and
that's why I'm here.
  (She looks at MARGARET, who ignores her.)

SHELLEY

Was it recent?

JEANNE

Last week.

MARGARET

Well, I think we may need to catch Shelley up on some
of what she missed.
  (To SHELLEY.)
Did they tell you anything about the first session?
  (SHELLEY, still staring at JEANNE, turns.)
Did they tell you what you missed?

SHELLEY

No.

MARGARET

"Focus."
  (Pointing with two fingers from her eyes to
  SHELLEY's eyes, the "focus gesture")

SHELLEY

What?

MARGARET

The subject of last week's session... "Focus."
(Repeating the gesture)

SHELLEY

Oh.

GOLDIE

Yes. Focus is very important. I took a lot of notes.
(Checking her notes)
You see, we mothers have really been trained in another
direction. It's not our fault or anything, but it's just that,
because we have had to change diapers, cook breakfast,
make the beds, see that the socks match—although I
don't do that, because, honestly, who is going to notice
the socks on a twelve-year-old boy—
(JEANNE glares at GOLDIE.)
—but, anyway, we have not learned to focus on the big
picture.

INDIRA

Can't see the woods for the trees...

MARGARET

Can't see the war for the bandages.

GOLDIE

Yes. That's just what the trainer said: Women can't see
the war for the bandages. So the first thing we have to
do is learn to focus on the right thing.

SHELLEY

(Intrigued)
And what is the right thing?

221

INDIRA

The rules of the playground.
    (She gestures toward the dryboard.)
This is a diagram of the playground.

SHELLEY

What playground?

GOLDIE

The one right here, right outside the windows... Where
we drop the children off.

INDIRA

And you can see that it's all divided up into 'safety
zones"—

MADELEINE
    (Interrupting, she turns to SHELLEY.)
Do you have a daughter?

MARGARET
    (Jumping in)
That doesn't make any difference.

GOLDIE
    (Anxiously, to SHELLEY)
That's right. Gender is not the issue.
    (To MARGARET, apologetically)
That's been one of the hardest attitudes to change.

MADELEINE
    (To SHELLEY)
Do you have a daughter?

INDIRA

Why are you asking her that?

MADELEINE

Because I think she ought to know.

SHELLEY

Know what?

INDIRA

(Quickly)

You ought to know that this program is one hundred
percent committed to eradicating stereotypes about
gender—

(To MADELEINE)

All stereotypes. There is no room in this program for any
misogyny *or* for any male-bashing—or any racism, anti-
Semitism, heterosexism—There is absolutely no room
for prejudice of any kind in the rules of the playground.

SHELLEY

(With visible relief)

Well, I'm all for that.

(To MADELEINE)

I *do* have a daughter, but I'm raising her to be a
feminist.

(She sits in the front row.)

MARGARET

(Ominously)

The trainer spent quite a little time last week talking
about feminism.

SHELLEY

That's wonderful!

INDIRA

I don't know if "wonderful" is the word. I mean, we're

INDIRA (cont'd)

grateful to the feminists for what they've done to raise awareness about inequality toward women—but their lack of political experience—which was not their fault—has led to a painful legacy of prejudice against males, so that now, two generations later, we are reaping the bitter harvest of those seeds of hatred planted by the feminists.

MARGARET

That's right.

GOLDIE

(Earnestly)

A lot of people want to blame violence in the schools on boys, but it's that very attitude that makes them act out.

SHELLEY

(Turning)

I don't understand. Isn't it mostly men who are fighting the wars and doing the raping and killing—

MARGARET

(Furiously)

Focus!

INDIRA

(Crossing to the board)

Okay...

(Tapping the board to get their attention)

The safety zones... These have been scientifically drawn up to address the inequalities inherent in any population of children—or adults.

SHELLEY

(Confused)

What do you mean?

INDIRA

Well...for example, this area here is considered one of the "preferred safety zones," because of the desirability of playing basketball. These...

(Pointing)

.... the monkey bars, the area with the trees, the picnic tables—these are all preferred zones also. Similar to, say, countries with oil fields. These preferred zones are on a rotation system. No one group of children can monopolize them.

SHELLEY

Wait a minute—what "groups" of children are you talking about?

GOLDIE

(Checking her handbook)

In this particular school, we have about 40% African American, 15% Latino, 35% European-American, and 10% "other." Now, the breakdown by income is 30% low income, 40% middle class, which would be, for a two-parent family, over $50,000 a year... Then, you've got the Catholics and the Protestants and the Jews—

SHELLEY

(To GOLDIE)

But I thought you didn't discriminate!

INDIRA

We don't. But we don't put our heads in the sand either. These are populations that have either common cultures, or who face common oppressions...*outside* the school, of course. And we want to honor their affinities and their cultural identities and acknowledge their disadvantages by assigning them their own safety zones on the

INDIRA (cont'd)

playground. And, as you can see...
    (Indicating the formulas)
...this is a complicated process. But we have a team of
some of the world's most experienced political analysts
and peacekeepers to instruct us in how to do that.

GOLDIE

Yes. The safety zones are the cornerstone of the whole
peacekeeping program.

MARGARET

Boundaries.

SHELLEY

But it sounds like the children can't play together...

INDIRA

No, no, no! The safety zones don't restrict them! They
just give them a power base from which they can learn
to negotiate shared use with others. For instance...
    (Pointing to the "Ethnicity Chart")
....today is Monday. As you can see on the "Ethnicity
Chart," the African-American students have the
basketball safety zone today.... Now, they can use their
temporary control of that area to negotiate with, say, the
Asian-American children for the use of the monkey
bars...or, with the European-American children for the
picnic tables...but, if they choose not to share—and
that's their choice—well, as you can see, tomorrow the
Asian Americans will have the basketball hoop and the
African Americans the picnic tables.

GOLDIE

On traditional playgrounds, with no safety zones, the
dominant group controls everything all the time.

INDIRA

We are giving everyone a piece of the pie right from the
start. They don't have to fight for it.

SHELLEY

But it's so complicated.... When are the children going
to have time to play?

MADELEINE

(Cryptically)
You mean, "fight?"

GOLDIE

(Hastily)
So how did your former school handle conflict?

SHELLEY

(To MADELEINE)
What do you mean, "fight?"

INDIRA

Yes, Shelley, how did your old school handle conflict?
This was one of the questions they asked all of us in last
week's workshop.

MARGARET

The one you missed.

SHELLEY

(Standing to address the group)
Oh.... Well, I guess we would give the kids "time out"
if they were being inappropriate.

MARGARET

(Sneering)
"Inappropriate!"

SHELLEY

(Confused by MARGARET's hostility)
You know, where you send the child off to be by
himself....

MARGARET

"*Him*self?"

SHELLEY

Yes.... Until he's ready to rejoin the others...

MARGARET

"He?"

INDIRA

Or "she."

GOLDIE

We used to have timeouts here, too, before the
peacekeeper program.

INDIRA

It's blaming the children.

SHELLEY

What is?

INDIRA

Timeouts.

SHELLEY

I don't understand.

GOLDIE

We have to *completely* change the way we think.

INDIRA

The timeouts and the locker checks and the detention
halls—these are just ways of scapegoating the children.
It's really *inequality* that's behind the violence. You
solve the problem of inequality and you remove the
motive for acting out.

GOLDIE

(Reading from the handbook)
"Timeouts and detention just humiliate the child, sowing
seeds of frustration and revenge that will yield a bitter
harvest of violence down the road."

SHELLEY

But what if the child is being inappropriate—

MARGARET

(Cutting her off)
Children are *always* appropriate.
(SHELLEY stares at her.)

GOLDIE

That's right. If we mothers don't like what they're
doing, it's up to us to locate the inequality that is the
source of their frustration and adjust the rules.
(She smiles.)
Focus.
(The "focus" gesture)

SHELLEY

What if whatever they're doing is just because they're
tired or cranky or because they saw it on TV—

GOLDIE

Oh, no! We can't blame TV!

SHELLEY

But there have been studies that television and video
games—

MARGARET

You can prove anything with studies. But if you really
want to solve a problem, you go to the experts.

INDIRA

And have we got experts! Listen... We've got folks here
from the Middle East, from Northern Ireland, from
Afghanistan...Rwanda...
    (JEANNE, still standing at the back of the
    classroom, kicks the trash can. The others turn
    to look at her. There is an awkward silence.)

SHELLEY

But do these rules of the playground really work?
    (JEANNE laughs. Another silence.)

INDIRA

(Uncomfortable with JEANNE's outbursts)
Well, it takes time for any new system to take root, but,
yes, absolutely. And at the end of the ten weeks of this
program, all of us here will be certified PDA's.

GOLDIE

"Playground Dynamics Analysts."

INDIRA

We will all be competent to evaluate what we see on the

INDIRA (cont'd)
playground and adjust the safety zones to respond to any crisis.

SHELLEY
You mean, you never discipline the children?

INDIRA
The PDA *observes*, but never interferes.

GOLDIE
(Reading from the handbook)
"It is imperative, in order to maintain neutrality, that the peacekeeper respect the process of all parties. The role of the PDA is limited to analysis and interpretation of violence, and allocation of safety zones."

SHELLEY
So you treat the playground as if it was the world, and the children represent all of the different nations competing for resources...

GOLDIE
Exactly!

SHELLEY
And the children will not be disciplined, because they will be treated like adults.

MARGARET
Discipline only humiliates them.

GOLDIE
(Reading)
"When you discipline a child, he or she internalizes the

231

GOLDIE (cont'd)
blame, which destroys the impulse toward social
justice."

SHELLEY
But if a child is getting hurt by other children—

MADELEINE
(Cutting in)
We let them do it.

MARGARET
(Attempting to divert attention from MADELEINE)
Focus! It's about focus!

SHELLEY
But what about the child?

MARGARET
I think it is really a mistake for anyone who missed that
first session to be allowed to join the program.

JEANNE
(Responding to SHELLEY)
That child should know how to fight.
(There is a silence, and then all the women begin
to speak at once.)

GOLDIE
That's not the point...

INDIRA
The big picture! We have to look at the big picture!

MARGARET

I don't see why they decided to set aside their own rules
to let someone...

MADELEINE

(Endorsing JEANNE)
That's right! That's right!

JEANNE

Quiet!
(The women stop talking. JEANNE crosses
slowly to the front of the class.)
My son is dead. Margaret's two boys killed him last
week while the blinds were down [curtains were closed]
and our international peacekeeping expert-of-the-day
stood and watched.

GOLDIE

(Nervous)
I think we should wait for the PDA before we try to
analyze what happened last week.

JEANNE

(Ignoring GOLDIE)
If my son had known how to fight, he'd still be alive.

MARGARET

I agree with Goldie that we are losing our focus.

INDIRA

I don't want to take sides, but it does seem to me that
we're doing exactly what the PDA warned would
happen if we stopped focusing on the rules of the
playground.
(Pausing)

INDIRA (cont'd)
We're taking the same sides that our children did.
(Just then a shot rings out.)

SHELLEY
(Alarmed)
What was that?

JEANNE
(Smiling)
Margaret lets her boys play with guns.

SHELLEY
(Aghast)
Real ones?

MARGARET
(To JEANNE)
I think it's a mistake for you to be here. You have
obviously lost your focus.

SHELLEY
What happened last week?

JEANNE
(Pleasantly)
Margaret's two boys shot and killed my son.

SHELLEY
(Struggling to make sense of what she is hearing)
You mean this is some kind of game—like paintball?...
Some kind of role-playing exercise... Is that what you're
saying?
(There is another shot, followed by a scream.)

SHELLEY (cont'd)
MARGARET shows some alarm. INDIRA is
strangely calm.)
Oh, my God! What was *that*?

JEANNE
(Calmly)
It sounds like one of Margaret's boys.

MARGARET
(Taking a breath)
Focus.

GOLDIE
(Confused)
It can't be one of Margaret's boys, because they're the
only ones with guns.

INDIRA
(Smiling)
No... Actually, my son brought a gun today.

SHELLEY
What are you talking about?

MARGARET
(Losing her composure, she turns on INDIRA.)
You gave it to him to use against my sons!

INDIRA
He wanted a gun, and I didn't want to interfere.

GOLDIE
(To MARGARET, gesturing with glee)
Focus!

MARGARET
(Regaining her composure, to GOLDIE)
It could have been your son.

GOLDIE
(Chin up)
Maybe.

SHELLEY
You're all crazy. This is a game...a test or something....
I'm going to look!
(She crosses to the blinds/curtains, but
MADELEINE steps in front of her.)

MADELEINE
No! We're not allowed to look out the window!

SHELLEY
Says who?

GOLDIE
It's the rules!
(SHELLEY attempts to open the blinds/curtains,
but MADELEINE grapples with her. The
blinds/curtains come partially open. There is
another, different scream.)

SHELLEY
That's my daughter! What are they doing to my
daughter?

JEANNE

Ask Madeleine.
     (MADELEINE says nothing.)
They raped her daughter last week.
     (Another scream.)

SHELLEY

Oh, my God!
     (Turning toward the women)
You're all crazy!

> She pulls away from
> MADELEINE and runs
> toward the door.
> MARGARET shoves a
> chair in front of her.
> SHELLEY crosses around
> it, but MARGARET has
> positioned herself in front
> of the door. SHELLEY
> stops for a moment, and
> then she picks up one of
> the chairs, as if to hit
> MARGARET with it.
> MARGARET steps to the
> side, and SHELLEY exits.

INDIRA

     (Her attention suddenly directed toward
     MADELEINE)
Did you bring Christy?

MADELEINE

     (Defiant)
No, I didn't.

INDIRA

That's not fair. We all made a commitment.
(Another shot.)

GOLDIE

(To INDIRA)
What about you giving your son a gun? Now *my* son is
the only boy who isn't armed!

INDIRA

It's not about gender and it's not about weapons.

MARGARET

That's right. It's about the rules of the playground.

MADELEINE

Why aren't there any safety zones for the girls?

INDIRA

It's not about gender.

MADELEINE

But girls are oppressed as a group. They're *more*
oppressed! They're the most oppressed group in the
school!

GOLDIE

God made boys the way they are! It's not their fault!

MADELEINE

(To INDIRA)
So why is it that these fancy-schmancy think tanks and
peacekeeping organizations never divide the map by
gender? Why don't the women of Ireland have their own

MADELEINE (cont'd)
country? Or the women in the Middle East? Why is it
the rules of the playground never take the war against
women into account?

INDIRA
You're talking like one of those 1970's feminists.

GOLDIE
It's because she's the only one of us with a daughter!

MARGARET
It's because she kept her at home! She's not really part
of the program anymore. She's broken the rules.

MADELEINE
You can't answer my question! Why don't the women
ever have their own base of power?

GOLDIE
(Hysterical)
It's the home! We already have one! We have the
babies! We don't need any more power! We can
negotiate with that! Every woman is her own nation!
(A round of gunshots. GOLDIE starts
screaming.)
My son! My son!

MARGARET
Focus! Focus!
(INDIRA grabs GOLDIE, who is trying to see
out the window. Another round of shots.
GOLDIE is screaming. MARGARET turns to
INDIRA.)
Close the blinds [curtains]!

INDIRA

I can't!

> More gunshots. GOLDIE
> breaks free and begins to
> run frantically between the
> door, which MARGARET
> is blocking, and the
> window that INDIRA is
> blocking. Finally, she
> collapses, sobbing and
> moaning. JEANNE
> watches her
> dispassionately for a
> moment, and then crosses
> to the windows, where she
> takes her time closing the
> blinds/curtains. She turns
> back to look at GOLDIE.

JEANNE

Goldie, I think you should have one of your brownies
while we all wait for the PDA.
      (Nobody moves. JEANNE picks up the brownie
      plate and extends it to MADELEINE.)
Madeleine, will you pass them?

> There is a long,
> meaningful look between
> MADELEINE and
> JEANNE. Slowly,
> MADELEINE crosses to
> the plate of brownies, and
> as she reaches out to take
> the plate from JEANNE,
> the lights fade.

(BLACKOUT)

THE END

Patricide

A Play in One Minute

Play Summary

Patricide is a one-minute monologue by a woman of any age, race, ethnicity, physical ability, sexual orientation, or class background who telephones her father and confronts him with her memory of his sexual abuse of her.

More than a novelty piece, this monologue provides actors with the opportunity to run an intense gauntlet of peak emotions in the space of sixty seconds: panic, terror, disorientation, relief, euphoria.

One woman
One minute
Bare or elaborate set, with telephone

Cast of Characters

<u>Woman</u>: A woman any age, any race, any ethnicity, any size, any class background, any sexual orientation, any degree of physical ability.

Scene

A place with a telephone.

Time

The present.

Patricide

Setting:	Any setting, or none at all, as long as there is a telephone.
At Rise:	The WOMAN enters. She stands or sits down by the telephone. Picking up the receiver, she dials a number.

WOMAN

Hello...Daddy?
    (Slight pause)
This is Carmen.
    (Slight pause)
Uh–hunh.
    (Slight pause)
It has been a while, unh-hunh.
    (Slight pause)
Two years, that's right—No. Wait! Daddy, I have something I want to say to you—I know. I—I know. And you can say what you have to say after I've said what I need to say—Da– Daddy. Listen. I have called you up, because I have something to say to you.
    (Slight pause)
What?
    (Slight pause)
No! No, I'm not willing to listen to you, until you hear what I have to say. If you can't listen then I'm going to hang up.
    (Longer pause)
I said I'm going to hang up if you can't listen to me.
    (Long pause)
Okay...

WOMAN (cont'd)
>(She takes a deep breath.)

I remember...
>(Another breath)

I remember that you...
>(Slight pause)

...sexually abused me.
>(Pause)

Hello?
>(She hangs up the phone, closing her eyes.)

I did it.
>(Opening her eyes)

I did it.
>(A long pause, as a smile begins to break on her face.)

Yes.

(BLACKOUT)

THE END

Jane Addams and the Devil Baby

A One-Act Play

Play Summary

In 1912, Jane Addams was witness to a strange phenomenon, as thousands of immigrants flocked to Hull House in response to the rumor that there was a "Devil Baby" there. The Devil Baby was supposedly an infant with hooves, horns, and tail. According to folk myths, this incarnation of the devil was the result of a drunken husband's curse that he'd rather see a devil in the house than another baby.

In this one-act, Jane confronts an elderly Irish woman who has broken into Hull House with the single-minded intention of gaining access to the Devil Baby. The woman is not to be deterred, and Jane matches wits with her in her attempt to find an explanation for this strange obsession which seems to have taken possession of half of Chicago.

Jane Addams and the Devil Baby is a radical confrontation between the sensibilities of a nineteenth-century, Irish emigrant wife-and-mother, and a progressive American lesbian of inherited wealth.

Three women
Twenty minutes
Single set

Cast of Characters

<u>Jane Addams</u>: A woman in her fifties.

<u>Mary Rozet Smith</u>: Jane Addams's companion lover.

<u>Kathleen</u>: A woman in her seventies.

Scene

The parlor of Hull House, Chicago.

Time

1912.

Jane Addams and the Devil Baby

Setting:	The scene takes place in the parlor of Hull House, in Chicago in 1912.
	The parlor is a large room, graciously furnished. There are many works of fine art on the walls. A large window opens into the room.
At Rise:	As the play opens, JANE ADDAMS is seated at a desk, trying to answer letters. JANE is fifty-two.
	A bell is heard offstage, and then MARY ROZET SMITH's voice.

MARY

(Offstage)

No.

(A pause.)

No. It's not here.

(Another pause.)

No, we didn't hide it. It's never been here. There's no such thing.

(Pause)

No. No. You can't come in and look. No. I'm sorry.

(JANE gets up and crosses to the window.)

No, it's not a question of money. You couldn't see it for five dollars, you couldn't see it for ten dollars, because it's not here. It doesn't exist. Good-bye.

MARY (cont'd)
(Another long pause and the bell rings again.)
What? No, you can't see it for twenty!
(The door slams and MARY enters the room.
She is a well-dressed woman.)

JANE

You should have taken the money. Hull House can
always use it.

MARY

Oh, I can see the headlines now: "Jane Addams
Swindles Chicago Poor in Devil Baby Racket." I'm glad
you have a sense of humor about it.

JANE

I don't have much choice.

MARY

I'm tempted to tell them that it's been moved to
Milwaukee. They'd sooner travel to Wisconsin than
believe me when I tell them it doesn't exist.

JANE

Look. Look out the window.

MARY

(She crosses to the window. Jane puts her arm
around her.)
I don't believe it! The streetcars are backed up for ten
blocks!

JANE

Pilgrims.

MARY

Why do they keep coming? We've turned everybody
away. Nobody's even gotten into the house. The
newspapers have reported that it's nothing but a rumor.
But still they keep coming. This is the third week and
there are more people every day. The doorbell rings
every five minutes. And they're all so sure it's here. They
can even describe it to me: the pointed ears, the tail, the
cloven hoofs. They tell me their sister-in-law has seen it,
or their mother, or the woman who works next to them
on the line. They're so sure it's here. Why?

JANE

That's the question. Why? And they're almost all
women. Some of them must be losing wages to take
time off from work. They seem to be willing to pay
almost any price to see it.

MARY

Yesterday a woman came and offered me her life
savings if I would show it to her.

JANE

(Crossing back to her desk)
Why is it so important for them to see it?

MARY

Because they're ignorant and superstitious.

JANE

I think it goes deeper than that.

MARY

Well, I don't. They're coming here the same way they
would walk three miles to look at a tenement that
collapsed, or a fire, or a cart overturned on the street. It's

MARY (cont'd)
just some kind of freak show for them. Anything morbid
to stimulate their curiosity.

JANE
No, I don't agree with you, Mary. I've been at Hull
House for twenty years, and every time I attributed
something to ignorance or superstition, I was always
wrong.

MARY
Don't tell me you believe there's such a thing as the
Devil Baby?

JANE
Well, Mary, take a look.
        (She gestures toward the window.)
If we don't, we're certainly outnumbered.

MARY
You can't be serious.

JANE
I am.

MARY
Do you mean to tell me that you believe the story that a
husband came home drunk one night, tore a holy picture
off the wall, told his pregnant wife that he would rather
have a devil in the house than a baby, and because of
that, her baby turns out to be some incarnation of the
devil—horns, hooves, and all? Are you saying that's
what you believe?

JANE
I believe there are many ways to see the world, Mary,

JANE (cont'd)

and those women lined up out there are seeing
something—or want to see something—that you and I
don't understand. Look at them. They're Italian, Russian,
Polish, Irish, Jewish, German. Some of them haven't left
their neighborhoods in forty years. Look at them.
They're coming on streetcars, on foot, on canes, in
wheelchairs. Most of these women have never had a
vacation in their lives. But here they are, streaming to
Hull House to see this famous Devil Baby they're so
sure we're hiding. These women are not tourists. No,
they're making some kind of pilgrimage. But why? What
is it about this Devil Baby that arouses such a passion in
them?

> (Just then the sound of the bell is heard,
> ringing insistently.)

I'll go.

MARY

No, I'll go. You try to get some work done. At least
something around here will be normal.

> The women kiss on the
> mouth, affectionately. She
> exits. JANE returns to her
> desk and picks up her
> papers.

> As she works, the window
> begins to open very
> slowly. An elderly woman
> dressed like a bag lady,
> crawls in through the
> window.

The woman,
KATHLEEN, is an Irish
immigrant. She is in poor
physical condition, but she
is possessed of an
unquenchable vitality of
spirit. A lifetime of living
by her wits has sharpened
her perceptions and given
her an uncanny ability to
read character.

JANE has her back toward
her and doesn't see her.
The woman makes a quick
inspection of the room and
then begins to creep
toward the hall door.
JANE notices her. She
rises from her desk and
begins to follow the
woman. She reaches the
door and begins to turn the
knob very slowly. The
door fails to open.

JANE

You have to lift the latch while you turn the knob.

KATHLEEN

(In a thick Irish accent)
That's kind of you to tell me.
(She starts to lift the latch, and then realizes she
has been discovered. She whirls around to face
JANE.)
Oh! Well, there you are. Why didn't you answer the

KATHLEEN (cont'd)

door? Well, now, I've gone and saved you the trouble of
letting me in.

(She pauses.)

I tried the door first, of course.

(She laughs.)

You don't think I'd be climbing in through a window
like some kind of heathen, if I hadn't tried the door first.
You must have been too busy with your work to hear me
knocking.

JANE

We have a bell.

KATHLEEN

Oh, do you now? And I'm a liar, aren't I? And a thief
too, no doubt. Well, why don't you just call for the
police now, and have old Kathleen arrested for breaking
into your house. I'm dangerous, you know. They call me
the Butcher of Halsted Street. I'm known to crawl
through the windows of rich ladies and slit their throats
while they're sleeping in their beds. I'd advise you not to
turn your back on me. That's a mistake you won't have
to make twice.

JANE

(Smiling)

What are you doing here?

KATHLEEN

Why, I'm here to murder you and take all your money, I
just told you.

(JANE laughs.)

And just what's so funny about that? No, I'll tell you. I
can see what you're thinking. I can see what people are
thinking, just as clear as you can see those pictures on

KATHLEEN (cont'd)
the wall. It's a second sense I've got. My mother had it
too. You're thinking I'm a fine one to be talking murder
when I'm standing here with one foot and four toes in
my own grave. You see, I know what people are
thinking.

JANE
I think you haven't told me why you're here.

KATHLEEN
(Ignoring JANE's remark)
But I want to tell you you're wrong. If you see an old
lady when you look at me, it's no accident. It's taken me
years and years to look this old...me whole life in fact.
Why when I was young, I couldn't look this old if me
life depended on it. No, it's not an easy thing to be this
old, and if I'd had a mind to die, I would have done it
years ago before I'd had to work this hard to stay alive.
After all this, you think I'm going to let the bastards get
me?

JANE
Are you here to see the Devil Baby?

KATHLEEN
Is it here?

JANE
I was asking the question.

KATHLEEN
So was I. Where is it?

JANE
Why do you want to see it?

KATHLEEN

I didn't say I wanted to see it, now did I?

JANE

No, you didn't.

KATHLEEN

Well, now. So don't go thinking you know what I'm thinking. Unless you have the second sight.

JANE

No, I don't have it, unfortunately. Well, since you're not here to see the Devil Baby, and you can't slit my throat unless I turn my back on you, which I'm not going to do, then I guess you'll just have to show yourself back out the window.
(JANE crosses back to her desk and goes back to work. KATHLEEN is agitated.)

KATHLEEN

(After a moment of indecision)
Well, now, supposing I was here to see the Devil Baby.
(JANE looks up.)
I'm not saying I am. Just supposing. How much are you charging people to see it?

JANE

I haven't said it was here, have I?

KATHLEEN

I'll tell you what, Miss Addams—you are Jane Addams, aren't you?

JANE

Second sight.

KATHLEEN

Well, Miss Addams, I'll strike a bargain with you.
(JANE looks attentive.)
I can see what you're thinking again. You're thinking
what does this poor old woman have that she thinks I'm
going to want. Now, am I right that's what you're
thinking?

JANE

You tell me.

KATHLEEN

I just did. But I'm a business woman, too, you see, and I
am going to make you an offer that no one else in
Chicago is going to match.
(She pauses dramatically.)
If you show me the Devil Baby, I'll bring five hundred
women to Hull House to see it, at one dollar a head.
That's five hundred dollars for showing me the Baby.
(She says the following with pride.)
Now...I don't know what you're charging to see it, but
I'm bound to say it to you—that's the best offer you'll
get.

JANE

How are you going to bring these five hundred women?

KATHLEEN

That's my secret.

JANE

How do I know they wouldn't come anyway?

KATHLEEN

Oh, you'll know.

JANE

How?

KATHLEEN

Because the women I'll be bringing aren't like any
others.

JANE

Who are they?

KATHLEEN

That's my secret.

JANE

I don't see how I can make this deal with you unless you
tell me.

KATHLEEN

Five hundred dollars. A woman could help a lot of poor
people with five hundred dollars.

JANE

If she knew where it was coming from.

KATHLEEN

You'll have to take my word. Five hundred dollars, take
it or leave it. That's a final offer.
   (JANE shrugs and goes back to work.
   KATHLEEN heads for the window. She climbs
   halfway out, but when she sees that JANE isn't
   looking, she turns and comes back into the
   room.)
They're invisible.

JANE

(Looking up)
What did you say?

KATHLEEN

(Impatient)
The women. The five hundred women. They're invisible.

JANE

I see.

KATHLEEN

No, you don't. You don't see much. But I do, and that's
why if you let me see the Devil Baby, I can bring you
these five hundred women.

JANE

Who are invisible.

KATHLEEN

That's right.

JANE

Is the money invisible too?

KATHLEEN

(Angry at being patronized)
Money's not invisible!
(She walks away shaking her head in disgust.)
"Is the money invisible?" When did you ever see money
that was invisible? You could put an old woman's body
out on the sidewalk, and just watch the people walk
around her like she was a pile of old rags. But just lay
two pennies over the poor women's eyelids, and see how
long they stay there. "Is the money invisible?" Let me
ask you something, Miss Addams—have you ever been

KATHLEEN (cont'd)

poor?

JANE

No.

KATHLEEN
(KATHLEEN snorts with satisfaction.)
Then half the world's a mystery to you.

JANE

That may be true.
(JANE rises.)
Kathleen, your five hundred women are old and poor, aren't they? They're women that are in the poor house, aren't they?

KATHLEEN

They'll pay a dollar, if that's what you're worried about. I give you my word.

JANE

But they're poor.

KATHLEEN

They're poor, but they'll pay.

JANE

What is it about this Devil Baby that makes a woman who can't even afford the wood to heat her room willing to come to Hull House and offer a life's savings to see it? What is it about this baby with the horns and the hooves that makes them so desperate to come?

                         KATHLEEN
          (A gleam in her eye)
Show me the baby, and you'll have five hundred chances
to ask that question.

                           JANE
I can't.

                         KATHLEEN
What do you mean, you can't?

                           JANE
I can't show it to you.

                         KATHLEEN
It's the money.

                           JANE
No.

                         KATHLEEN
How much do you want?

                           JANE
It isn't the money. I can't show it to you, because it isn't
here.

                         KATHLEEN
You've hidden it.

                           JANE
No. It isn't here.

                         KATHLEEN
You've moved it.

                           266

JANE

No. There's no such thing. It doesn't exist.

KATHLEEN

Now I know you're lying.
     (She pulls out a knife and holds it to
     JANE's throat.)
There is a Devil Baby and you'll show it to me!

JANE

     (Surveying her calmly)
No.

KATHLEEN

The games are over, Miss Addams. There is a Devil
Baby, I know, because my great-great grandmother saw
one, and she told my mother. There was a man in her
village whose wife had given birth seven times to little
girls, and he cursed her eighth pregnancy, saying he'd as
soon have a devil in his house as another girl, and she
birthed a Devil Baby. And my great-great-grandmother
was there at the christening, when they unwrapped the
baby and it started to curse, and jumped down and
chased the priest all over the church. Don't tell me
there's no Devil Baby, when my own great-great-
grandmother has seen it!

JANE

You can look for yourself.

KATHLEEN

Oh, and wouldn't that be a fine thing—and while I'm off
on a goose chase, you call the police on old Kathleen.
No, Miss Addams, you and me are going to see that
infernal baby together, or not at all. Get up.

JANE

It's not here.
>(KATHLEEN looks at her.)
It's not here.

KATHLEEN

>(She looks doubtful for a moment, and then
>rallies.)
You're lying.

JANE

No, I don't lie, Kathleen, and if I did, I would tell you
the Devil Baby is here in Hull House, but it isn't.
>(KATHLEEN sits.)
Put the knife on the table.
>(KATHLEEN looks at her.)

KATHLEEN

There's no Devil Baby at Hull House.

JANE

No.

>KATHLEEN puts the
>knife on the table and
>begins to cry. JANE puts
>the knife in a drawer and
>watches her.

KATHLEEN

The bastards! They've got everything! They've got
everything! The bastards...they've got everything.
>(JANE reaches her hand out to KATHLEEN's
>shoulder.)
Seventy-eight years. Seventy-eight. And they've got
everything. Everything.

268

KATHLEEN (cont'd)
(KATHLEEN sobs some more, and then she
becomes quieter. She looks at JANE.)
There's never been a Devil Baby, has there?

JANE

No.

KATHLEEN

(Nodding)
Ah. Those clever bastards. They've gone and got away
with everything.
(She smiles at JANE.)
Do you know what I live for? Just once—just once to
see them get what's coming to them. And I thought with
the Devil Baby, it was finally going to be their turn. But,
of course...nothing again. Me climbing out the window
of the poor house, having to beg a ride on the streetcar,
and then having to beg the driver to help me up and
down, and me with no fare! And all for nothing, again.
Those bastards. I bet you it was them that started the
rumor in the first place. That would be perfect.

JANE
I don't understand. What would be perfect?

KATHLEEN

The joke. The perfect joke. That a poor woman, married
off at thirteen to some drunken shiftless pig who used
her like a piece of filth for thirty years and kept her
having babies half her life while he's drinking up the
money—and her not even being able to take her own
children and or keep her own wages—and every night
him swearing and striking at her and the little ones—and
all these years her praying on her knees for the soul of
her husband and the life of her babies and the strength to

KATHLEEN (cont'd)
get up in the morning—and what's to show for it, I ask
you? The babies, they die anyway, and the ones that
don't, they grown up as good as dead. The girls taking to
living on the streets, and the boys getting themselves
taken off to jail, and in the end, the husband drinking
himself to death. And now her, too old and too poor to
start over. A lifetime of work and a body half dead with
carrying and nursing babies. Now, I ask you, where did
all those prayers go? Up the chimney like smoke? And
there's not even a Devil Baby to show for it.

JANE
So the Devil Baby is an answer to prayer?

KATHLEEN
To see just once in the flesh—for all the world—in the
flesh!—the living incarnation of the father's sins visited
on the children. Oh, a dozen times I could have birthed
that devil. I have. I have. A son who steals from his own
mother. Who takes the bottle just like his father? Who
comes after his own sisters like he was some kind of
animal? But where's his hooves and his horns to let the
world know it's not his mother's fault? It's the man, it's
the father in him spawned the devil! But who is it that
pays? The mother! The poor suffering mother.
  (She turns sharply to JANE.)
You've never had a husband?

JANE
No.

KATHLEEN
Then you can't know anything about a woman's life.

270

JANE

I'm sorry.

KATHLEEN

It's cruel, that's what it is. It's a cruel joke, this Devil
Baby.

JANE

It seems to be.

KATHLEEN

Well, it's not your fault. You don't know anything about
it.
    (She rises.)
I'll take my knife back now. It's the only one I have for
cutting bread, when I've got the bread to cut.
    (JANE retrieves it from the drawer and hands
    it to her. KATHLEEN takes it thoughtfully.)
You know, this is the first time I ever used a knife
against a living soul. I should have done it years ago.
    (She turns to go.)

JANE

You can use the door.

KATHLEEN

    (Turning)
Miss Addams—you teach a lot of girls at Hull House,
don't you?

JANE

Yes.

KATHLEEN

Teach them there's no Devil Baby. Teach them not to
wait for it.

271

She holds up the knife to
salute JANE who opens
the door for her.
KATHLEEN exits, and
JANE stands watching her
as the lights fade.

(BLACKOUT)

THE END

Battered on Broadway

A Vendetta in One Act

Play Summary

Nellie Forbush of *South Pacific* is in Mame's Manhattan penthouse to host a benefit luncheon to build a Broadway battered women's shelter. Her guests include Bess of *Porgy and Bess*, Julie Jordan of *Carousel*, Sally Bowles of *Cabaret*, Mei Li from *Flower Drum Song*, Maria from *West Side Story*, and Aldonza from *Man of La Mancha*. These women, most of them now older, look back in horror on their various onstage rapes, batterings, and partnerings with inferior men.

Orphan Annie, no longer so little, puts in an unexpected appearance and is outraged to discover that Daddy Warbucks has donated ten million dollars toward the shelter. She tells Nellie that when the reporters arrive, she will expose him as a child molester. Nellie is concerned that this will jeopardize the project. She threatens to have Annie arrested if she doesn't leave. Sally Bowles intervenes, and Annie is in for a surprise when the nun reveals her secret identity and initiates Annie into the mysteries of an underground vigilante group.

Battered on Broadway is a theatrical tour-de-force, combining the farcical romp of comic strip characters with the conventions of an old-fashioned murder mystery in a plot which rewrites the history of American musicals from a feminist point of view.

Ten women
Thirty-five minutes
Single set

Cast of Characters

Nellie Forbush Debecque: from *South Pacific*

Bess: from *Porgy and Bess*

Mei Li: from *Flower Drum Song*

Aldonza: from *Man of La Mancha*

Maria: from *West Side Story*

Julie: from *Carousel*

Sally Bowles: from *Cabaret*

Orphan Annie: from *Annie*

Maid

Nun

Setting
The setting is Mame's Manhattan penthouse.

Time
The time is late morning, the present.

Setting:

The scene takes place in the living room of Mame's lavish Manhattan penthouse.

NELLIE FORBUSH DEBECQUE is hosting a reunion for women from former Broadway hit musicals. Most of the women are in their fifties or sixties, depending on their age in the musical and the year the musical opened.

The women are: BESS from *Porgy and Bess*, MEI LI from *Flower Drum Song*, ALDONZA from *Man of La Mancha*, MARIA from *West Side Story*, JULIE from *Carousel*, and SALLY BOWLES from *Cabaret*. There is a NUN present, presumably Guinevere from *Camelot*.

At Rise:

The women are standing around in groups, laughing and talking.

The MAID enters with a

coffee service and begins
to pour. NELLIE checks
her watch, and dismisses
the MAID.

NELLIE
(Clinking her spoon against her cup)
Ladies! Ladies… May I have your attention, please?
(They give her their attention)
Thank you. I think we're ready to begin here. First I'd
like us to introduce ourselves, and then Julie here is
going to talk about the project that we're here to
organize. Let me say, it's wonderful to be back here in
New York, and it's so wonderful to see all of you again -
after so many years. I think it's been twenty years since
I saw you, Bess.

BESS
Thirty, honey. But when the reporters get here, we'll tell
them twenty.

SALLY BOWLES
When is the press going to arrive?

NELLIE
In about a half an hour. I thought we could all get
through our business first, and then they could join us
for the luncheon buffet and take candid shots during
that. I know how we all hate this kind of invasion, but I
think it's really important for the success of our fundraising that we have this kind of publicity. But anyone
who doesn't want to be interviewed or photographed can
leave before they get here.

ALDONZA
Who is coming?

NELLIE

Time, *Life*, *Newsweek*, the *Washington Post*, the *New York Times*, and all three major networks...and "All Things Considered."

BESS

Didn't leave anyone out, did you?

NELLIE

Not if I could help it.

JULIE

Are they all going to fit in here?

SALLY BOWLES

In Mame's penthouse? Are you kidding? She used to invite half of Manhattan to her parties.

BESS

That's the truth. Where is that girl anyway?

NELLIE

She's off exploring the Himalayas with Vera, but she's very supportive of the project. That's why she loaned us her penthouse for the reunion.

BESS

The Himalayas! Mame must be in her eighties!

SALLY BOWLES

She wanted to do them before she got too old.

NELLIE

Well, let's start with introductions. I'm Nellie Forbush DeBecque, from *South Pacific*.
(She turns to JULIE)

JULIE

And I'm Julie Jordan from *Carousel*.

BESS

Bess from *The Sound of Music*.
(They all laugh appreciatively.)
No, wait—*Porgy and Bess*. With all the Black musicals
they have on Broadway, I keep getting it confused.

MARIA

Maria from *West Side Story*.

SALLY BOWLES

(Giving herself a "Joel Grey" introduction)
Fraulein Sally Bowles! From *Cabaret*. And this is my
friend Guinevere from *Camelot*. Guinny has taken vows
of silence, you know.
(The NUN bows in acknowledgement)

ALDONZA

I am Aldonza, la prostituta from "El hombre de la
Mancha."

MEI LI

Mrs. Wang Ta, formerly Mei Li from *Flower Drum
Song*.

NELLIE

It's just wonderful to see all of you here today. And I
know some of you have had to travel quite a distance to
be here—Guinevere and Sally have flown in from
London, and Aldonza from Spain. Mrs.Ta lives in San
Francisco.... I know what an effort you have all made to
be here, and I'm grateful for your commitment to the

NELLIE (cont'd)

project. And now I'm going to let Julie tell you about
that, because it was her idea.

JULIE
(Rising, she speaks to NELLIE)
Thank you, Nellie. If it weren't for your help in
organizing the reunion, I couldn't have done it. I'll never
know how you managed to track down everybody after
so many years.
(To the others)
But there's one woman we couldn't invite today, and
that woman represents why we're here. I'm sure we all
remember Nancy Sykes.
(There is a murmur of assent)
Nancy is not here today, because Nancy is dead. She
was beaten to death by her husband, onstage, in the
musical *Oliver*. Those of us who saw it opening night
will never forget it.
(Pause)
Nancy's death should not have been a surprise. It had
been coming for a long time. Not many people will
remember, but I was also a battered wife. It didn't
happen onstage, like with Nancy, but I talked about it. In
the second act my daughter came to me because her
father had hit her, and I told her that when some men hit
you, it feels like a kiss.
(The women respond with shock.)
And for those of us who were not actually battered in
our shows, we were surrounded by it. I think of Anna in
The King and I. Every other woman in that play was in
sexual or domestic slavery to the king of Siam. And how
was she supposed to react? She taught him ballroom
dancing! How many of us were expected to give up our
dreams and ideals to meet the selfish desires of
worthless men—men who represented the opposite of

281

JULIE (cont'd)

everything we stood for. What happened to Marion in
The Music Man? All she wanted was a quiet, gentle
partner who could talk to her about Shakespeare. What
did she get? A traveling salesman who made his living
by selling nonexistent band instruments to children! And
Sarah from *Guys and Dolls*, a woman committed to
fighting a war on alcoholism and gambling addictions...
Who did she have to marry? Skye Masterson—a
professional gambler and an alcoholic. And Liza
Doolittle—spunky little Liza...she closed her own show
by fetching slippers for her master like some kind of
dog. Nellie?

NELLIE

My story is a familiar one, too. My first taste of freedom
was also my last. I was away from home for the first
time, supporting myself, living in a wonderful
community of army nurses—having the time of my
life—and what happens? I'm supposed to want to give it
all up to go live on a plantation with a man twice my
age, and raise his children for him!

ALDONZA

(Facetiously)
Pobrecita!
(MARIA laughs. NELLIE is surprised and
offended.)

JULIE

(Making peace)
All of us here know what it is to be victimized by a
script that is written from the point of view of rich white
men. We know what it is to say lines that betray
ourselves, to give up our lives to serve inferior men, to
participate in our own abuse. We know that we did these

282

JULIE (cont'd)

things not because we were stupid, not because we were
masochistic, not because we wanted to. We did them
because we had to. We did them because we had no one
to turn to, nowhere else to go. Nancy Sykes died,
because she had no support in her efforts to save Oliver.
If there had been some shelter where she could have
gone, Nancy would be with us today. This is why I
would like to see us, victims of Broadway's earlier
misogyny, raise the money for a Broadway Battered
Women's Shelter.
    (The women applaud. Suddenly the bell rings.)

NELLIE

I'll get it, Julie. You go on.
    (The MAID enters, but NELLIE waves her away.
    She lingers at the tea table, eavesdropping.)

JULIE

I feel this is an opportunity for me to correct the damage
done by my role in *Carousel*. I feel that this is a chance
for me to do something for the younger women who are
coming along now...
    (NELLIE has received a telegram and is
    reading it.)

NELLIE

Wait, Julie! Listen!
    (She reads.)
"I regret that my daughter will be unable to attend your
luncheon..."
    (SALLY makes eye contact with the MAID.)
"...Am wiring ten million dollars to your account. Hope

NELLIE (cont'd)
this will be of some service to the Battered Women's
Project. Best of luck."

    (SALLY crosses to the MAID, whispers to
    her, and the MAID exits.)

JULIE
Ten million dollars…

SALLY BOWLES
Who's it from?

NELLIE
Daddy Warbucks.

BESS
That man has got money.

JULIE
He's the richest man in the world.

SALLY BOWLES
I wonder why Annie didn't respond herself.

NELLIE¶
I don't know, but this is certainly a windfall.

MARIA
Does this mean you don't have to raise any more
money?

NELLIE
This will cover the cost of buying the site and building
the shelter. We would still have to raise the funds for
operating expenses. I'm sorry, Julie. I'm afraid I
interrupted you.

JULIE

No, I was just finishing up anyway. I would like to get some feedback from the rest of you about the project.

BESS

Sounds like a good idea to me. I came up here with that pimp Sportin' Life, and an armful of drugs. Took me ten years to get clean and get free of that bastard.

ALDONZA

You were a prostitute?

BESS

A working girl, honey.

ALDONZA

Don't be ashamed of it. I was a prostitute. Today in Spain I organize the girls who work in the sex trades. We are not ashamed. We work for our money, and when we have it, it's our own. Where's the shame?

MEI LI

I was a mail-order bride.

ALDONZA

You see? You show me the women who don't have to suck dick to live, and then I will be ashamed to be a prostitute.

MARIA

Lesbians.

ALDONZA

What about lesbians?

MARIA

The women who don't have to sell themselves to men.

ALDONZA

Don't tell me that! Half of the prostitutas are lesbians.

MARIA

My lover and I, we don't work for men. We don't live with them, we don't go out with them, we don't talk to them. We don't have anything to do with them.

ALDONZA

So where does your money come from?

MARIA

We have a karate school for women, and we publish a magazine for Latina lesbians.

ALDONZA

And with this you make big money.

MARIA

Not big money. But we can live.

ALDONZA

To live! Women want more than just to live! We want our cars. We want our houses. We want some good clothes for the children. We want to eat well. Maybe even go to a restaurant every now and then. Buy a few flowers. To live! To live with nothing is sucking on the dick!

MARIA

No, it's not!

ALDONZA

Don't tell me! They gonna stick it to you one way or
another. Don't tell Aldonza about fairy tales. Tell them
to Dulcinea. Don't' tell them to Aldonza!

BESS

We have to start somewhere. And the reason we're here
is the battered women's shelter, right Nellie?

NELLIE

That's right. I was thinking…

ALDONZA

(Interrupting, to MARIA)
Maria! Maria! What happened to your cousin?

MARIA

My cousin?

ALDONZA

The one they tried to gang rape on the stage. It was
inside a store…with the white boys…you know, the Jets?

MARIA

You mean Anita?

ALDONZA

Si, Anita. How is she?

MARIA

She's dead.

ALDONZA

Did she kill herself?

MARIA

No. It was an overdose of heroin.

ALDONZA

She killed herself.

BESS
(Putting her hand on MARIA's arm)
That's hard.
(There is a long silence.)

ALDONZA
(Singing)
"Little bird, little bird/ In the cinnamon tree/ Little bird, little bird/ Do you sing for me?"
(No one says anything. They recognize the song.)
That's the song they sang when they gang-raped me onstage. Big party. Big men. I spit on them. I spit on the Jets.
(She spits. The doorbell rings.)

NELLIE

Excuse me a minute.
(The MAID enters again, but NELLIE arrives at the door first and opens it. ANNIE stands there, a woman in her thirties with wild red hair and sunglasses.)

ANNIE

Is this the Broadway reunion?

NELLIE

Yes...and you must be...?

ANNIE

(Taking off her hat and her sunglasses and
tossing them to the MAID, who takes them,
looks at SALLY, and exits.)
Annie. As in "Little." As in "Orphan."
(She sweeps into the room.)

NELLIE

We understood you weren't coming.

ANNIE

Who told you that?

NELLIE

We got a telegram from your father.

ANNIE

My father? Warbucks is not my father. Let's get that real
straight right now. He bought me. Like he buys
everything. He was my owner, not my father.

NELLIE

Well, he sent a telegram saying you weren't coming.

ANNIE

Yeah, he wished. He had me all locked up snug in a
private institution—paid them to keep me there. But two
can play that little game. I paid them to let me out.

SALLY BOWLES

Why did he lock you up?

ANNIE

Why? Because I'm crazy—can't you tell? And I'm not
cute anymore, or hadn't you noticed? Little Orphan

289

ANNIE (cont'd)
Annie has grown up. She doesn't wear spanky pants
anymore. And she talks.

SALLY BOWLES
So Warbucks had you locked up for no reason?

ANNIE
Oh, he had reasons. He had plenty of reasons. And today
I'm going to tell the whole world all about them.

NELLIE
What do you mean?

ANNIE
The press is going to be here, aren't they?

JULIE
Yes.

ANNIE
Good. Good! How do I look? I don't want to look crazy,
you know. I thought this little outfit would have just
enough softness to make me look vulnerable, but not
enough to make me look frivolous. What do you think?
You know how it is with first impressions.

NELLIE
I'm sorry, Annie, but I'm not understanding what it is
exactly that you're planning to do here.

ANNIE
I am planning to tell the reporters the truth about Daddy
Warbucks, Daddy Bigbucks, Daddy Bumfucks. I'm
going to tell them just why a rich white man who's in
the business of making war, takes such an interest in

ANNIE (cont'd)
rescuing little orphan girls. I'm going to tell them just
what it is he does with his little sugar and spice
investments.

ALDONZA
So Mr. Warbucks fucks little girls?

ANNIE
(Looking at her)
I couldn't have said it better.

SALLY BOWLES
(She reaches out to touch ANNIE. ANNIE
whirls around with her fists up.)
I'm sorry, love. That must have been awful!

ANNIE
Don't feel sorry for me. I'm going to get my revenge.
After today, the whole world is going to know the kind
of man Warbucks is.

SALLY BOWLES
That could be very dangerous.

ANNIE
What could he do to me now? I've grown up. I'm a free
woman. I have my own money. What could he do?

SALLY BOWLES
He could have you sued for libel. He could threaten your
friends. He could have you locked up again. Actually,
there's a lot of things he could do.

ANNIE
He wouldn't dare. The whole world will be watching.

NELLIE

Annie, I'm concerned that you want to use this benefit
for your press conference. We're here to talk about
building a battered women's shelter on Broadway.

ANNIE

And I'm here to talk about why we need one.

JULIE

But your story is so sensational, it's going to
overshadow the news about the project.

NELLIE

That's what I'm thinking. I'm thinking it would be
better for you to hold your own press conference.

ANNIE

No, you don't understand. I can't plan one without
Daddy finding out and canceling it. No, this is perfect.

NELLIE

Well, I'm afraid I don't agree with you. This is not the
right place for you to tell your story. We want the focus
to be on the shelter...It's a separate story from your
experiences with your father.

ANNIE

He's not my father.
    (Looking around)
What? Do you hear this? I can't believe it! What the
fuck is your shelter about if it isn't about my story?
Where could an orphan girl go? And now you're telling
me it's not related!

JULIE

I think what Nellie means is that we're here to save women, not to accuse men.

ANNIE

Say what? And just how do you expect to do that? If you've got a battered woman—*somebody* did the battering. How are you going to save women if you don't accuse men?

NELLIE

There are law courts for that. We are just interested in raising the money for a shelter—giving the women a place to go.

ANNIE

For what? So they can rest up for round two? So they can stop short of mental breakdown or death and go back to the abuser? The men are going to love that. You know what you're talking about? A recycling center for abused women. How nice. How convenient. I bet you could even get Daddy Warbucks to donate a chunk.

    (An embarrassed silence)

JULIE

Actually, he already did.

ANNIE

    (Outraged)
What?

JULIE

He already donated.

ANNIE

How much?

MARIA

Ten million.

ANNIE

(To NELLIE)
You're not going to take it?

NELLIE

I...We didn't know...We'll have to discuss it.

ANNIE

(To the others)
You're not going to take it! You're not going to build
your shelter with Daddy Warbucks' money!

JULIE

Ten million dollars will buy and build the center, Annie.
Real estate in Manhattan is very expensive. It would
take us years to raise that kind of money.

ANNIE

Well, it's going to be pretty interesting explaining that to
the press after I tell them about his child molesting.

NELLIE

Annie, I don't think that's a good idea.

ANNIE

And I don't think taking his money is a good idea.

NELLIE

These are two separate issues.

ANNIE

What about the rest of you? Do you think these are
separate issues?

MARIA

I think we all feel your pain, Annie.

MEI LI

You have suffered a terrible wrong.

BESS

No one's arguing about that.

ALDONZA

That's why we take his fucking money. As long as the women have to suck dick, we will make the men pay for it! We will make them pay a lot of money!

ANNIE

No! You don't understand. Ten million dollars is nothing to Warbucks. It's chicken feed.

NELLIE

But it's not chicken feed to us, Annie.

ANNIE

Exactly. And that's what men like Warbucks count on. They can always buy us off.

JULIE

We're not saying you should protect him. I think you should tell the press your story…

MARIA

File a lawsuit!

JULIE

…It's just that you shouldn't tell it here today.

ANNIE

You're wrong. If I don't tell it here today, I may not
have another chance.

NELLIE

I understand your feelings, but I hope you will respect
ours.

ANNIE

No. Because you're wrong.

NELLIE

(After a silence)
Then I will have to ask you to leave.

ANNIE

No.

NELLIE

Then I will have to call the security guard in the lobby
and have you removed.

ANNIE

Go ahead.

JULIE

Annie, we're on the same side.

ANNIE

No, we're not. I'm on my side. You're on Warbucks'
side.

JULIE

How can you say that?

NELLIE

Don't argue with her. I'm going to buzz security.
(She rises.)

SALLY BOWLES

Wait!
(NELLIE turns.)
Let me talk to Annie for a minute—in private.

ANNIE

Nothing is going to change my mind.

SALLY BOWLES

I know that, love. I just want a minute alone with you—
that's all. I know you're going to do what you're going
to do.

NELLIE

I'll wait in the dining room.

SALLY BOWLES

(To others)
Can you all wait with Nellie for a bit? Won't be long, I
promise.
(They murmur assent and exit.)

MARIA

(Lingering)
Guinevere, are you coming?

SALLY BOWLES

(To the NUN)
I'd like it if you stayed, actually.
(The NUN nods.)

ANNIE

What? Is she going to pray for me? Or maybe for
Warbucks?

SALLY BOWLES

(To MARIA)
I'll join you in a minute.

MARIA

Annie, I want you to know you can call me if you need
to talk to someone.
    (ANNIE turns her back to MARIA. MARIA
    starts to leave. She turns back with a final appeal
    to ANNIE.)
You can call me anytime.
    (She exits.)

ANNIE

(After a moment)
So. You're going to lecture me about being realistic.

SALLY BOWLES

Annie, do you know who this is?
    (She indicates the NUN.)

ANNIE

It's Guinevere from *Camelot*, isn't it?
    (The NUN removes her glasses and her veil.)

SALLY BOWLES

Do you recognize her?

ANNIE

No. *Camelot* was before my time.

SALLY BOWLES
This isn't Guinevere. It's Nancy Sykes—from *Oliver*.

ANNIE
I thought Nancy was dead.

NUN
(Looking at SALLY, the NUN breaks into a
powerful and raucous laugh, relaxing into a
butch pose. When she collects herself enough to
speak, it is with a Cockney accent.)
That's what they all think.
(She laughs again.)
I've been waitin' a long time to meet you, haven't I,
Sally?

ANNIE
Why don't you tell them you're still alive?

NUN
Because I've got more freedom bein' dead.
(Explosive laughter. The NUN punches SALLY,
who is enjoying the joke.)

SALLY BOWLES
Do you know why she came here today?

ANNIE
No.

SALLY BOWLES
Because of you, love. All because of you. Nancy wanted
to talk to you.

ANNIE
I don't understand.

NUN

We've had our eye on Warbucks and his gang for a long
time.

ANNIE

You have?

NUN

He's behind the dirty little games in Nicaragua and
Chile. He's the dodgy bastard who's been Enron. It was
his little tinker toys that made the accidents at Chernobyl
and Bhopal. No, I can tell you, Warbucks has been a
very busy little boy.

SALLY BOWLES

Due for a spanking, he is.
     (She and the NUN laugh.)

ANNIE

     (Interrupting their joke)
Well, today the world is going to hear the truth about
him.

NUN

The world is not going to hear the truth about him.

ANNIE

Yes, it is. And no one can stop me. If they throw me out
of this building, I'll wait on the street for the reporters. I
am going to tell my story. No one can stop me.

NUN

No one can stop you, dearie. No one can stop you at all.
But just because you tell it, doesn't mean anyone's
going to hear it.

ANNIE

Why won't they hear it?

NUN

Because they can't afford to hear it. Like you said
yourself, Warbucks owns everything. People who have
his money are scared of losing it, and people who don't,
are scared they won't get it. They won't hear you until
they have a good reason to hear you.

ANNIE

So you don't think I should do anything?

SALLY BOWLES

Let Nancy talk.

She touches ANNIE's arm
again, and again ANNIE
spins around, prepared to
fight. Suddenly the MAID
enters with a pot of tea
and a cup. She makes a
long, deliberate cross to
the NUN, pours her a cup,
crosses in front of
ANNIE, and stands by the
tea table.

NUN
(Smiling at the MAID)

Bill Sykes, me lovin' husband, beat me to a bloody raw
pulp in *Oliver*, and he left me for dead. If it hadn't been
for my girlfriend who came lookin' for me, I would have
died. It was she who took care of me all those months
while I was decidin' whether or not it was worth it to
live. Do you know, I had to learn to walk all over again.

NUN (cont'd)

I had to learn to talk. Couldn't remember a single bloody word for anything. Do you know who it was taught me English again?

>(ANNIE doesn't answer. The NUN points to the MAID.)

May I present Liza Doolittle?

ANNIE

Liza Doolittle! From *My Fair Lady*?

MAID

>(Bowing, she speaks with a Cockney accent also.)

At your service.

NUN

Liza is a mistress of many disguises—and many voices. After I was on my feet again, the first job we pulled was Higgins' house. Cleaned the blighter out, we did. Took all his language books and records…

MAID

Took his bloody slippers, too.

ANNIE

He didn't know?

MAID

Oh, he knew all right. He was just too proud to report that his little human experiment had backfired on him. You know his male ego.

NUN

And then we set up shop, so to speak. Whenever we'd hear about women who'd been raped or robbed or beaten up, we'd go trackin' down the bloody bastards.

ANNIE

Would you kill them?

NUN

Let's just say they disappeared.

ANNIE

You kill men?

MAID

We save women.

ANNIE

Yes, but...you could go to jail!

NUN

How? Liza here's always in perfect disguise, and I'm already dead!
(She explodes in laughter.)

ANNIE

What about Sally?

SALLY BOWLES

I've got the money, love.
(The three conspirators share a laugh.)

ANNIE

But . . . you were in Berlin . . .

SALLY BOWLES

I left Berlin during the war, and I came back to London.
I couldn't go back home to Mummy, you know—the
tears and all of that muck—and I felt so guilty about the
things I'd seen while I was sleeping around with those
Nazi officers—well, I was feeling quite blue, actually.
So one night, when I was walking by the Thames, I just
took a notion to end it all, as they say. I was just taking
my shoes off to jump, when this woman reaches out and
grabs my arm, like this.
    (She laughs.)
It was Nancy.

NUN

We'd been watchin' her, of course, since she came back.
We knew she'd be very helpful to us.

SALLY BOWLES

You see, I knew a lot of Nazi secrets.

MAID

She knew where Hitler was hiding.

ANNIE

You mean you killed Hitler?

SALLY BOWLES

He killed himself, actually.

NUN

With a little persuasion.

MAID

They all kill themselves, don't they? That's how we see
it. By the time they've made our list, they've become so

MAID (cont'd)
selfish and destructive, we don't consider them human
anymore.

SALLY BOWLES
Anyway, to make a long story short, this whole business
with the Nazis was terribly exciting, and I stopped being
depressed, and I realized that I didn't want to kill myself
at all, but I really just wanted to kill men. I've been
working with Liza and Nancy ever since.

ANNIE
So what do you want with me?

NUN
We want to help you.

ANNIE
You mean expose Warbucks?

SALLY BOWLES
Dispose Warbucks.

ANNIE
You want to kill him?

NUN
Don't you?

ANNIE
No...I mean...I don't think… No. That's too much.

MAID
(Crossing in close to ANNIE)
How many lives has he ruined?

ANNIE

I don't know. Hundreds, I guess.

NUN

And how many more is he going to ruin?

ANNIE

(She pauses.)

A lot.

SALLY BOWLES

(Crossing in to ANNIE from the other side)

Then we really can't allow him to live, can we, love?

ANNIE

(Jumping away from SALLY and the MAID)

You're crazy.

(The NUN looks at SALLY. SALLY reaches
out to touch ANNIE's arm. This time, ANNIE
lets herself be touched.)

No, I'm sorry I said that.

SALLY BOWLES

(Putting her arm around ANNIE)

It's all right, love. It's a crazy world.

NUN

Good women get killed because they're too good to
fight back. Good women pray, good women sign
petitions, good women march for peace. Meanwhile
their sisters are gettin' raped, their planet's bein' sold
out from under them for scrap, and their children are
gettin' blown to bloody bits. You see, we've stopped
bein' good women.

MAID

But we're effective, Annie. Very effective.

SALLY BOWLES

We'll need a lot more information on Warbucks and his friends before we can act. We have plenty on him, but we need more about his operation.

NUN

We need you to go home again. To pretend to get along with him. We'd like you to hire a new secretary for your Daddy.

MAID

Someone with a strong background in languages.

NUN

It's going to take a bit of time, but we always guarantee satisfaction.

SALLY BOWLES

Work with us, Annie. We need you.

ANNIE

(After a pause)
Yes... Yes.

SALLY BOWLES

(Embracing her)
That's a girl. You won't regret it. Besides, it's rather fun.

NUN

The world will thank you.

MAID
I'd better practice my typing.

SALLY BOWLES
Well, now that's all settled, I'll tell Nellie we're through in here.
>   (The MAID hands the NUN her sunglasses and head covering. The NUN puts her disguise back on.)

Nellie!

NELLIE
>   (Appearing)

Yes?

SALLY BOWLES
Annie here has changed her mind. She's decided to leave before the reporters get here.

NELLIE
Oh, Annie, I'm so glad you understand our position. This is really for the best.

ANNIE
Yes, I can see that now.

SALLY BOWLES
Good girl.

ANNIE
>   (To NELLIE)

Good luck building your shelter, any way you can.
>   (To the NUN)

And bless you, sister.
>   (The NUN crosses herself.)

NELLIE

Thank you, Annie. Good luck to you, too. I hope you can get some good therapy.

ANNIE

(Smiling)

The best.

(She exits.)

NELLIE

Well, Sally, I don't know how you did it. I was afraid we were going to have to have a very unpleasant scene on our hands.

SALLY BOWLES

Oh, don't thank me. It was our Gwynny here did the miracle.

NELLIE

But how?

SALLY BOWLES

(Shrugging)

The meek shall inherit the earth, don't you know?

(BLACKOUT)

THE END

Postscript for *Entr'acte*

Within three years of the rape, Eva Le Gallienne left Broadway at the height of her fame to found her own theatre company, the Civic Repertory Theatre. It became one of the most famous theatres in the world. She leased an old theatre at 14th Street near 6th Avenue, in Greenwich Village—where the lesbians lived. She hired lesbians as actors, as fund-raisers, as administrators, as directors, as designers.

The Civic, according to director Bobby Lewis who apprenticed there, had the reputation of being a lesbian theatre. It was well-known that Eva lived upstairs with her lover Jo Hutchinson. Many of the young women and girls in the apprentice program were lesbians, including young May Sarton and including Glesca Marshall who would become the life partner of lesbian actress Alla Nazimova, a role model of Eva's who eventually came to work at the Civic, starring in *The Cherry Orchard*. Gladys Cathrop, one of the set designers, was one of Eva's lovers, as was costume designer Irene Sharaff. According to Lewis, a considerable portion of the audience for the Civic was also lesbian. The theatre was located a few blocks from a lesbian nightclub called The Cosmic where Spivy, a lesbian singer, would, after her set, cook breakfast for the after-theatre crowd of dykes from the Civic.

Eva's company performed true repertory, sometimes presenting as many as five different plays in rotation during a single week. No actor was expected to take on the persona of a character for months—or even years, at a time—as was the case with Broadway theatres. In keeping with Eva's vision of a democratic theatre, all of the Civic's work was offered to the public at popular, non-Broadway prices.

Eva selected all of the plays herself, choosing work that featured strong roles for women, with a marked absence of the ingenues and masochists of the traditional canon. She performed the role of Hedda Gabler, the Ibsen heroine who chose suicide over sexual blackmail and imprisonment in a stultifying marriage. She also realized a lifelong dream to play Hilde Wangel in Ibsen's *The Master Builder*. As Hilde, Eva wore boys' clothes and confronted the old man who was sexually inappropriate toward her as a child. Exploiting his narcissism, Eva as Hilde challenged him to his death. She played Peter Pan with a highly original portrayal of him as a deeply disturbed, pre-adolescent boy. She cast her lover, Josephine Hutchinson as Alice in *Alice in Wonderland*, while she herself played the White Queen who believes six impossible things before breakfast.

And, speaking of impossible things, Eva intentionally sought out the work of women playwrights. She was the first to produce Susan Glaspell's Pulitzer-prize-winning play *Alison's House*, a play with a thinly disguised plotting about poet Emily Dickinson and the need to tell the truth about the sexual lives of famous women. She also commissioned lesbian author Clemance Dane to write a play about suspiciously spinsterish Jane Austin.

Eva Le Gallienne, who, after the rape, would go out of her way to avoid Broadway, may have made a connection between her physical violation in the dressing room and the context in which that violation occurred. She may have realized that she had been in an entire system that supported that violation. She had been playing a woman who defended her batterer in a play that romanticized violence against women. She had been in a male-dominated theatre that was all about making money, at the expense of the art and the artist. The system of long-runs, especially for young actresses in ingenue roles was deadly in terms of developing acting skills. And there would be no roles at all for actresses when they moved into their middle years, even though some of the greatest roles for male actors were written for men in their prime. The actress who went along with this system would find herself out-of-work and facing financial ruin as she reached her mid-thirties.

The Civic Rep created previously unimaginable employment opportunities for women where they were paid salaries equal with the men in an environment free of ageism, looksism, and sexual harassment. In fact, Eva hired Mimsey, her now-married ex-lover, to come work for her as an administrator. For five years they would work side-by-side, their offices next to each other. In providing her lover Jo Hutchinson with steady income, Eva empowered Jo to leave her husband and come live with her.

Eva understood the need to create her own environment, one in which male dominance in any form would not be tolerated. She recognized the need to feel as free about her sexuality as heterosexual actors, and she could only do this in a theatre she could control. Eva, proud of her lesbianism and referring to herself as "ahead of her time," refused to hide behind the facade of a heterosexual marriage, as did fellow lesbian actors Katharine Cornell and Lynne Fontanne.

Eva's work attracted the attention of bisexual First Lady Eleanor Roosevelt, who met with her privately to determine her needs. Shortly after that, President Roosevelt offered Eva the directorship of the Federal Theatre Project, an opportunity that promised to rescue the Civic Rep from the ravages of the Depression. Eva turned him down. She was too savvy not to know that in this proposed union of interests, the government would be the husband and the art would be the wife. She rightly surmised that the price of this paternal subsidy would be her hard-won artistic freedom. She lost the

Civic Rep, but she never regretted her decision. (She also paid a high price for her financial autonomy, when Jo Hutchinson's husband named her as the co-respondent in the divorce. The case was widely publicized and may have been a factor in Eva's decision not to take her cross-dressing, summer-stock Hamlet to New York.)

The rape and the breakup with Mimsey, both deeply traumatic events for Eva, appear to have been catalysts for her founding of the Civic Repertory, a radical experiment in theatre that holds a place in history for its original vision, uncompromised artistic standards, empowerment of women, and public accessibility.

Printed in the United States
204953BV00002B/44/P